Out of chaos comes the most beautiful moments.

Crystal Smith

Beautiful Chaos

Our Story about Foster Care, Adoption, Faith, and Love

Crystal Smith

WESTBOW PRESS®
A DIVISION OF THOMAS NELSON
& ZONDERVAN

Copyright © 2018 Crystal Smith.
Interior Graphics/Art Credit: Elissa and JR Smith

All rights reserved. No part of this book may be used or reproduced by any means, graphic, electronic, or mechanical, including photocopying, recording, taping or by any information storage retrieval system without the written permission of the author except in the case of brief quotations embodied in critical articles and reviews.

NIV: Scripture quotations marked (NIV) are taken from the Holy Bible, New International Version®, NIV®. Copyright © 1973, 1978, 1984, 2011 by Biblica, Inc.™ Used by permission of Zondervan. All rights reserved worldwide. www.zondervan.com The "NIV" and "New International Version" are trademarks registered in the United States Patent and Trademark Office by Biblica, Inc.
NLT: Scripture quotations marked (NLT) are taken from the Holy Bible, New Living Translation, copyright ©1996, 2004, 2007, 2013, 2015 by Tyndale House Foundation. Used by permission of Tyndale House Publishers, Inc., Carol Stream, Illinois 60188. All rights reserved.
WEB: Scripture taken from the World English Bible.

This book is a work of non-fiction. Unless otherwise noted, the author and the publisher make no explicit guarantees as to the accuracy of the information contained in this book and in some cases, names of people and places have been altered to protect their privacy.

WestBow Press books may be ordered through booksellers or by contacting:

WestBow Press
A Division of Thomas Nelson & Zondervan
1663 Liberty Drive
Bloomington, IN 47403
www.westbowpress.com
1 (866) 928-1240

Because of the dynamic nature of the Internet, any web addresses or links contained in this book may have changed since publication and may no longer be valid. The views expressed in this work are solely those of the author and do not necessarily reflect the views of the publisher, and the publisher hereby disclaims any responsibility for them.

Any people depicted in stock imagery provided by Getty Images are models, and such images are being used for illustrative purposes only.
Certain stock imagery © Getty Images.

ISBN: 978-1-9736-1978-9 (sc)
ISBN: 978-1-9736-1979-6 (hc)
ISBN: 978-1-9736-1977-2 (e)

Library of Congress Control Number: 2018902109

Print information available on the last page.

WestBow Press rev. date: 03/06/2018

To my children, Sierra, Devin, Elissa, JR, Alex, Eli, and Sadie. Thank you for giving me such a beautiful story to write about. I love you more than all the moons and stars in the sky.

To my husband, Todd, thank you for believing in me and in our ever-changing family. There is no one I would rather share this journey with. After all, what's one more? I love you.

And mostly I thank God for allowing us to be His hands and feet for a few of His children. Thank You for Your unending love and blessings. To You, oh Lord, be all the glory.

To all of those who have asked, "Why haven't you?" or suggested I should write a book about our experience in foster care and with adoption through foster care, here you go. I hope you enjoy our story. May this book inspire others, maybe even you, to take a leap of faith and become foster parents.

Today is like any other day at the house. Our five-year-old daughter is sitting at the table hard at work on her ABCs. Three out of four boys are running around playing with the numerous cars and airplanes we have collected over the past few years. Our oldest son is still at marching band practice, while our oldest daughter is away at college. The phone rings. It's my husband, letting me know he will be a few minutes late getting in from work; there's an early run in the morning, and his boss asked him to stay late to help load the trucks. Our newest addition to the house, a tiny four-week-old baby girl, is sound asleep in her crib. There are dishes in the sink that need to be washed and clothes in the rocking chair that need to be folded. The living room floor is covered with wooden puzzle pieces and Legos.

Looking at the house, it's hard to believe I once had to have everything in its proper place, to the point that some people even thought I had OCD. At one point in my life, I made sure all the books were in alphabetical order on the bookshelf and that the clean clothes were put away promptly after being washed. Friends would say you could eat off my floors because they were always freshly mopped. Nowadays, if the books are on the bookshelf and not strung across the floor, I am grateful. As for the laundry, it seldom makes its way out of the clean-laundry basket. And I'm sure you could still eat off my floor; there's bound to be Pop-Tart crumbs, fruit snacks, or a few potato chips laying around somewhere. My priorities have changed. I have changed.

It's time to start dinner while the little ones are distracted by the cartoons on TV. Thanks to Mickey Mouse, I will have about thirty minutes to make a quick dinner that I'm sure only a few will eat. This is our life. This is our beautiful chaos, as we have named it. Never dull, never boring, always changing, and always busy. This is our story. This is how we became a forever family through foster care—our journey, step by step, as it unfolded, through the ups and downs of foster care all the way through the wonders of adoption. It's a story about our faith in God and how He guided us every step of the way. Our story is not a journey many people understand and even fewer choose to take, but it was the journey God chose for us. Every child, every tear, every smile, and every fear has made us the family we are today. This is how our family came to be.

Three Plus One: The Start of Our Story

Family is not an important thing, it's everything.
—Michael J. Fox

My husband, Todd, and I attended the same high school. Our school was one of the smallest in the county; less than nine hundred students walked the narrow hallways back in those days. We are part of the graduating class of 1994. We had many of the same classes and ate on the same lunch schedule. He played football, and I sang in the show choir. We were good friends, but it never turned into anything more. I had a steady boyfriend throughout high school, and because of that, Todd never asked me out. He was content with being my best guy friend.

We lived in a small town outside of Charleston, West Virginia. Back in the early nineties, there were no stoplights or fast-food restaurants in our town, and everyone that was anyone hung out at the local Go-Mart. Today, we have two stoplights, and both a Wendy's and a McDonald's. Go-Mart is still the place to meet up with friends; some things never change. As with many rural towns, life was simple and carefree back then. Friday nights were played out on the high school football field, Saturday's were spent cruising up and down the road in front of the high school, and Sunday mornings were spent in church. It was a place where you could walk down the road and the owner of the local grocery store would run you a tab; everyone knew their neighbors, and it was safe for children to play outside after dark. It was that kind of town.

Todd and I went through our four years making the most of our high school experience. We shared laughs, gave each other dating advice, and shared the occasional English and history assignment answers. Before we knew it, we were walking across the stage to receive our diplomas. We said our goodbyes and went on with our lives in separate directions. He worked a few odd jobs before joining the military, and I found myself pregnant at eighteen and married at nineteen. Todd and I would not see each other or talk again for fourteen years. Looking back now, it amazes me how God's big plan unfolded for us.

Our story picks back up in 2008, the year I found myself divorced.

In 1995 I was a newlywed college freshman with a baby. I had no clue what real life was. The first few years, to the outside world, I had a happy marriage and even welcomed my son into the world in 1998. But things were not always happy behind closed doors. In October 2000, my life went from bad to worse. That's when the car accident happened, the day my life was rearranged. I was on my way to my parents' house to pick up some clothes for my children. My aunt and uncle had invited them to spend the weekend at their house. There was oncoming traffic, so I was stopped waiting for the cars to pass by before cutting across the road into my parents' driveway. The driver of the truck never saw my car. By the time he looked up, it was too late for him to stop; he plowed into my Cavalier. He tried to swerve so he would miss me, but by doing so, he came up my side of the vehicle. There was nowhere for me to go. I remember the loud sirens of the fire trucks and police cruisers. The ambulance arrived and took me to the hospital. The whole incident is a blur. My world and my life forever changed.

My back and neck were seriously injured. The nerves in my left hand no longer worked. Over the next few years, I endured countless injections in my back, neck, legs, arms, and even my throat to relieve the pain. I spent months relearning how to hold a pencil and then how to write. The pain was unbearable, and the fear of not being able to care for my children was overwhelming. After a few years of trying different injections to relieve the pain without much success, in 2004 I had my first major surgery. It was to place a SCS (spinal cord stimulator) in my abdomen to relieve the pain in my neck and arms. Six months later, I had a second SCS placed in my lower back to relieve the pain in my back and leg. My kids playfully called me robot mom. Both surgeries were successful. My marriage, however, was a different story. It was falling apart quickly.

My marriage example was not what I wanted my children to use as to what a healthy marriage was supposed to be. I did not want them to base their future relationships on what they saw in our home. As my marriage crumbled, I knew I needed to get us away from the increasingly dangerous situation. Leaving was the easiest and the hardest decision I have ever had to make. I was raised in church and took my wedding vows seriously; however, I knew that if I stayed, things would only get worse.

So, in late February 2008, I took my children and left the only life I knew. With help from a few family members, I was able to move into a townhouse large enough for the three of us. Thankfully, it was in our school district, which meant the kids would still be able to attend their schools. They would deal with enough changes stemming from the divorce. Changing schools and leaving their friends was not something I wanted for them. Their schools, friends, and teachers provided a little bit of normalcy in their now upside-down world.

My life was broken, my body was broken, and so began the next chapter of my life, whether I was ready or not. What in the world was I going to do now? I had two choices: I could let the divorce and the past dictate every future decision, or I could overcome them both and be a survivor. The choice was clear; I had to survive. I had to move forward, if not for myself then for my children. But I was scared. I was used to being alone most nights, but this was different. We were on our own. Completely on our own. Just the three of us. We were all scared of the unknown, of what the future had in store, but two things were certain: we were safe, and we were together. The three of us had each other, and that was all that mattered.

My focus was my children. Only my children. They were the reason I had found the courage to start my life over. They were the reason I woke up in the mornings those first few months after the divorce. They were the reason I decided to take online classes to work toward my degree, which I had started years earlier. Everything I did was for them. It's always been about them. At that point in my life, I had no intention of dating or even talking to anyone. For years, I had been told I was not pretty enough or good enough, and I believed it. I felt beaten down, unwanted, and ugly. And if all of that wasn't reason enough, I felt a little old to be dating. Let's face it. I knew nothing about how to date in my thirties. The last date I had been on, I was fifteen. Who would date someone like me? Who would date someone with kids? I know that sounds crazy to some, but at the time, that's what was going through my mind. Little did I know God was working on something far bigger than I ever imagined.

A few months passed, and the kids and I were adjusting well. We were getting used to our new normal life. The kids were in a routine: going to school, going to taekwondo practice, going to church, and going on trips with their grandparents. Overall, we were making the best out of a tough situation. My main goal was to keep their lives as normal as possible. This desire to be normal led my daughter, by this time a teenager, to come home one day from school and ask for a MySpace account. I was not the most computer-savvy mom around, but I agreed to consider it. I had heard of MySpace; I just needed to make sure it was safe for her to use. After a few days of research, I agreed she could have a page only if I could monitor it (yes, I was and still am a helicopter mom). So, we each made an account. She added me as a friend, and all was great. I even added a few close friends and family members to my account. I was still dealing with my divorce, so it was easier to lie and say, "I'm doing fine," over the computer than in person. Somedays it was just easier not to face people.

One day after checking up on my daughter's page, I scrolled through some suggested profiles and stumbled across a page for my old high school. Our senior class president had set up a reunion page, so people could talk about and give suggestions on upcoming events. Can you guess who I found on that page? If you guessed Todd, then you would be correct. At least, I thought it was him, but years had passed, so I wasn't completely sure. So, just like a teenage girl, I sent him a message saying something like, *Hello, I think we had English together. If you remember me, it would be great to catch up, so add me. If not, ignore this.* Yes, ladies and gentlemen, that was the line that started our beautiful chaos. How crazy is that? He did respond, quickly I might add, and we had a good laugh. We started sending messages back and forth, and over the next few weeks, we caught up on life events as if fourteen years had not passed us by. It was nice having an old friend to talk to.

Meanwhile, my daughter was trying to get me to date or at least get out and meet people. She was tired of seeing me, as she put it, unhappy. Todd had also asked if we could go out or if he could meet my kids. I told them both no. I did not want a relationship; it felt too soon, and I was afraid it would mess up our lives. Besides, I was completely fine with our new normal. However, my daughter was not taking no for an answer. She had a friend whose parents had a friend who everyone agreed I had to meet. He was single, had a motorcycle, and was recently back from serving over in Iraq. Every woman's dream, right? Sierra insisted I meet up with him and at least go out to dinner. I turned her and her friend's parents down time after time. My heart told me if I was going to go out on a date with anyone, it was going to be with Todd. After all, we had been talking—well, messaging—back and forth. Plus, I felt like I knew him since we had gone to school together. He seemed to be the safest choice, not this motorcycle-riding soldier everyone was eager for me to go out with. I finally broke down and told Sierra that I had been talking to someone on MySpace. I went on to say that he had asked me to go out to dinner, but I had told him no. I wanted to make sure she and her brother were okay with it first. Both of my kids started giggling. They were excited that mom had "found a man" on the internet. They could not believe it. The idea that I was talking to someone brought about many questions from both of my children. They wanted to know who he was, what was he like, did he have kids, what kind of car did he have, and where did he live. All normal questions to ask a mom that just announced she was talking to someone off the internet.

To help answer some of their questions, I walked them over to the computer and pulled up his profile to show them Todd's picture. As I was doing so, I explained to them we had been friends back in high school, justifying to myself and them that it wasn't like I would be going out with a stranger. When his profile finally loaded, Sierra burst into laughter. She was laughing so hard tears started running down her face as she yelled, "That's him! That's the guy I've been trying to get you to go out with!" She was all smiles and immediately called her friend to tell her the news. My heart was strangely at ease. What were the chances of that happening? I mean seriously, what were the chances? Chance had nothing to do with it; it was God, all God. Only He could work out our paths so that we could be reunited, and only He would provide me multiple affirmations that I was doing the right thing. I still find it funny how God used social media and my daughter to bring Todd and me back together. He can use anything to make His plan happen. After my daughter calmed down, she and I sent Todd a message letting him know that I would love to go on a date with him.

On our first date, Todd included my kids. His friend had a boat, and we went out to watch the fireworks on the river. It was nice to see him face-to-face. Our friendship picked up right where we had left off. He confessed that back in high school he had a crush on me but never acted on it because I had a boyfriend. He then said now that I was divorced, and fourteen years had passed, he finally had the courage to ask me out. We both laughed. He still makes me laugh. Our old friendship grew into love, and one day in early August 2009, we became husband and wife in a small church service in our hometown. Sierra was my maid of honor, and Devin walked me down the aisle before taking his place as Todd's best man. On that day, we became a family—our three plus one.

Todd had never been married or had children of his own, but he was a natural at becoming a father to Sierra and Devin. He loved everything about being a dad. The kids adored him and loved spending time with him. In his eyes, he was never their stepfather; he was just dad. From the very start of our relationship, he was everything I had wanted in a spouse for myself and in a father for my kids. If you didn't know our background, you would have assumed that Sierra and Devin were his kids. I was blessed to have found someone who was not only willing to love me for me but who was also willing to raise children who were not his own. He did not have to; he chose to, and that spoke volumes to me.

Not long into our marriage, I started dreaming about another child. Todd had walked right into fatherhood of a preteen and a teenager. He missed out on all the little things like diaper changes, late-night feedings, the smell of a newborn in your arms, all the things new parents get to do. I felt guilty I could not give him that. Circumstances that unfolded in my first marriage left me unable to have more children. My heart broke for him, but he did not complain. He understood and told me not to worry. Our life went on with just the four of us.

I have learned over the years that God always has a plan for our lives. Many times, we do not see it coming, but He will find a way to make His plan a reality.

I was cleaning the house one day when I received a call to babysit. I had known the mom since she was a little girl, and just a few weeks prior to the call, I had gone to the hospital to visit when her baby girl was born. I jumped at the chance to watch the newborn. I soon became her regular babysitter. We loved having her over and did not mind watching her when her mom asked. After a few weeks, though, we noticed something was not right with the situation. At first, we would have the baby a day or two, then it went to three or four days. Without going into too much detail, let me say some things happened, and we ended up being awarded temporary emergency custody of the baby girl. This did not please everyone in the baby's family, seeing that I was an outsider, but the judge thought it best for the baby at the time. I didn't want to make anyone angry; I just wanted to help both the mom and the baby the best way I could. If that meant having the baby live with us, then she would live with us. We all wanted what was best for them, and I was willing to do whatever it took to make sure that's what they received.

We loved having the baby at our home. There's something about having a baby around that makes a house happier. However, from the beginning, we knew that reunification was the plan both the judge and her mom wanted. The young mom worked hard and completed all the necessary things ordered by the judge to get her daughter back. It was a long, hard road, but a few days before baby girl turned a year old, the court granted reunification, and she moved back in with her mom. It was a good day. I was so happy for the two of them. A few days later, we all celebrated baby girl's birthday together in their new home.

A lot happened during the time we had baby girl in our care. I was working toward my associate's degree in human science and was right in the middle of doing my final research paper when she went back to her mother. Maybe I was just missing having a little one running around the house, but everywhere I looked, I came across something talking about foster care. I knew the need for foster care parents was great in our area, but I was not sure it was something we could do. The news was full of stories about drug overdoses, child neglect, and child abuse. My heart went out to those children involved, but I did not want to expose my children to such horrible things. I finished my paper and placed the thoughts of foster care in the back of my mind. But God has a way of placing things in front of us for a reason.

I finished up my associate's degree and contemplated working toward my bachelor's degree in social work. I had always wanted to work with children, and I prayed that one day my back and neck problems would be manageable enough to allow me to go back to work. I wanted to be prepared if that day ever came. After looking at some colleges, the idea of foster care resurfaced. One night while lying in bed, God spoke to me. His voice was so clear, as if He was standing right in front of me. I still get chills thinking about that one-sided conversation. I jumped out of bed and woke my husband up. I told him about my experience with God just moments before and how God said to me, "My child, I have shown you what some of My children go through; I want you to house them, love them, protect them, and you will be rewarded with My blessings." The logical side of me was thinking, *There's no way God's plan for me is to be a mother to His children*. What did that mean anyway? How was I to care for other people's children when there were days my back hurt so bad I could not get out of bed? But I knew God wanted us to follow Him. I knew He was calling me to do this. Sometimes God takes us out of our comfort zones and makes us rely on Him and Him only. Without even questioning my sanity, Todd looked at me, took my hand, and said, "Let's do it." Later that morning, after the kids woke up, we sat down with Sierra and Devin and asked them what they thought about us becoming a foster family. Our kids thought it was a great idea, so, as a family, we made the decision to become part of the solution. We were to become a foster family. Our path was set. Let our journey begin.

Taking the Classes

For I know the thoughts that I think toward you, says
Yahweh, thoughts of peace, and not of evil to give
you hope and a future. You shall call on me, and you
shall go and pray to me, and I will listen to you.
—Jeremiah 29:11–12 (World English Bible)

I started doing research immediately. When God speaks, you listen. I considered which agency would be the best for us and what we would need to do to become certified, all while getting excited thinking about how soon we could be helping kids. After a few days, I called the local DHHR because that seemed to be the best place to start. The receptionist transferred me to a very sweet lady who oversaw the foster care training program. She was happy to help us get started and answered many of the questions I had. As "luck" would have it, she said there was a PRIDE training class starting that Saturday, and a few couples had dropped out. She stated that if we wanted, she could let us have one of the open spots and we could get started. I called Todd and told him about the class. He agreed we should start as soon as possible and made plans to get off work. Just like that, we were on our way to becoming foster parents. I truly believe if you are doing God's work, He will always make a way for things to work out. I do not believe in luck or chance; this was all by God's grace. His grace never ceases to amaze me. We told the kids as soon as they got home from school. They started picking up their rooms and cleaning out old toys and things they no longer needed. This was going to be a family effort.

Before we knew it, Saturday morning arrived, and it was time for our first class. We were told the training would take five weeks (or five Saturday mornings) totaling twenty-five hours. Training was held at a local college inside one of the medium-sized lecture halls. The room consisted of four off-white walls, a tile floor, one large table up front, and several individual student desks. It smelled of burnt coffee and doughnuts along with some strong perfumes and aftershaves. There were thirty people in our class. Some looked nervous, while others looked aggravated at the fact they had to be there at eight thirty on a Saturday morning. The instructor was a sweet, kind soul. I could tell right off she was passionate about foster care and the children in the system. She welcomed us all to class with a warm smile and gave us her background and why she had started teaching the training classes. She then asked us to give a little background on ourselves and why we had decided to become foster parents. We discovered that we were all there for the children, but we all had a different reason.

A few in the class wanted nothing to do with the fostering process. They wanted to adopt a baby or child because they were unable to have a child of their own, and they had heard adopting through foster care was less expensive than private adoption agencies. Some wanted to adopt a child to help expand their current family and had heard foster care was one way that could happen. Still others were there because someone in their family, maybe a son, daughter, sister, or brother, had lost custody of their children. Not wanting the family to be broken, they agreed to step up to be a "kinship" foster placement for the children. Most of the people in class, however, were there to be foster parents, meaning they did not necessarily want to adopt. They just wanted to help provide a safe place for a child in need if they could. They wanted to open their homes, to be a safe place for children to go and be loved until the child's mom or dad could get off the drugs, get out of jail, or get the services they needed to get their children back. This is where Todd and I fell in. Adoption would be great if it happened, but we really wanted to just help like we had with my friend's little girl. We wanted to be that couple who was willing to be there, to be that stable place for a child when his or her world was falling apart. We wanted to make a difference in a young child's life. The emotions were flooding the classroom as each person gave the reason they were there, and in that moment, I knew we had made the right call. Thirty people, thirty assorted reasons for being there.

At first, I thought having to take the classes was a little silly and unnecessary. After all, I was a mom. I knew how to raise a child. But over those five Saturdays, we covered topics I never imagined I would have to deal with, let alone knew anything about. Class could be on everything from basic hygiene to drug use, bedwetting, or swearing. We talked about sexual abuse, death, child porn, skipping school, low test scores, runaways, and teen pregnancy. The list went on and on. We talked about the legal side of foster care, what the different lawyers' titles meant, what a GAL (guardian ad litem) was, how often MDT (multidisciplinary teams) meetings were held, what took place at the MDTs, how long the process typically took, and a list of legal terms, some that I still to this day don't understand. We were told what we could do, such as enroll them in school or enroll them to play sports. We were also told what we could not do, such as cut their hair or pierce their ears. We could take them to the doctor, but we could not give permission to put the child to sleep for a procedure or surgery (only a caseworker could give permission for those types of things). We covered topics that should be common knowledge, like not allowing the child to use drugs in your house, keeping a curfew, making sure they are doing their homework, and ensuring they are fed. The different lists seemed endless.

One of the main topics in class was what the CPS (child protective service) workers call the seventy-two-hour window. This is the first seventy-two hours after a child comes into state care.

Once a child is in state care or the worker knows the child is being removed, the home finder on call must find a safe place for the child to stay. This could be in the care of another family member, a bed in a group home, a bed in a treatment center, or a temporary placement in a foster home. After the child is placed, the new care provider or foster parent has seventy-two hours to get the child to a doctor for a complete checkup. The sooner the better. In West Virginia, there are several forms that need to come with the child, such as a medical waiver form, a clothing voucher (if it's the child's first time in state care), a new medical card number, an emergency contact form, and a life book. Other states may differ on what forms are brought at drop-off time. Also, in this time frame, the new foster parent must make daycare arrangements if they work outside the home, set up a visit to WIC (Women, Infants, and Children, a food and nutrition service), and maybe even set up a dental appointment. The caseworker will inform the new foster parent of any upcoming MDT meetings or court hearings normally when the child is dropped off. We learned quickly that many children coming into care do not have the best medical records, so it is important for the foster parent to ask questions and search for answers.

The life book is a way to help foster parents keep up-to-date information on their new foster child. There are forms for medicine lists, behavior charts, lists for what the child came into care with, a medical background sheet for information on the parents if it is available, and even a place to add photos of the child. It is also important for the child to have. The book acts as a record of where they have been. It holds their story, the same as a baby book does for a newborn. In my years of experience, I have found the life books very helpful. The down side to the life book is that many people do not take the time to fill them out, or they get lost moving from one home to the next. We were told if the child did not come with a life book to purchase a notebook and write down important life events and add a few pictures when we could.

The classes were better than I anticipated. So much information was discussed that I had never really thought about. I had lived in a fairy-tale world. I had no idea that some children were subject to so much negativity and pain. Most of the children in foster care had seen or been through more than anyone should ever have to go through: abuse, neglect, drugs, homelessness, starvation, or dealing with a parent in prison. Their young lives had been forever changed by the bad choices someone else made. Their past would make them in many ways different from our children, but they were still kids, and they needed someone to believe in them, to love them. Someone that was supposed to protect them and love them had now disappeared, leaving them to pick up the pieces. Countless stories, sad and unimaginable stories, all broke my heart. Children forced to raise their younger siblings, children shaken so badly they died, children being made to have sex with strangers, so their parents could afford drugs, and their own drug use just to survive. Haunting scenarios like these were told over and over. No child should have to live like that or be forced to see those conditions. I would come home after some of the classes and just hold my kids. I would tell them just how special they were and how much I loved them. In my mind, all children were loved and protected by those they lived with. The reality was that many children lived a nightmare and prayed daily for a way out. I knew we could not save them all, but if we could help just one, maybe the world would be a better place. At the very least, that one child's world would be a better place.

Class moved along nicely. We got to know many of the people and their stories on a deeper level as time went by. We were fingerprinted and had background checks completed. We were given forms to fill out; in a sad way, they reminded me much like forms to buy a car. They were long and complicated and wanted to know every detail about us. They needed to know how many people currently lived in our house, where the house was located, did we have city water or well water, did we have gas heat or electric. There was a section on our finances: how much money did we make, how much did we have in savings, how much were our vehicles worth, and did we have a

401K? We had to give personal references of people who knew us so that the department could call and ask them if they felt we would be good parents. There were face-to-face interviews done with some of our references, while others answered questions through emails. The process was long and draining, but we were told it would help determine who would be the best foster care candidates. I guess if you are not willing to put in a few hours' worth of work to fill out paperwork, then chances are you would not be willing to deal with or capable of handling a child that cries for two hours straight.

After all that paperwork was finished, there was even more paperwork. This part was about what type of child we would consider for placement. I thought this would be easy; after all, they were kids. But this list was intense, very intense. There were pages containing questions like what race we would prefer, what age range we were looking for (newborn to two, newborn to five, five to eight, eight to thirteen, thirteen and up), if we were open to all ages, and if we would prefer boys or girls. Page after page of medical conditions and terms, many of which I had to look up because I had never heard of them. Still other questions like, Would we consider a child that's missing a leg(s) or missing an arm(s)? Would we consider a child with special needs? If yes, would we be open to a moderate need, mild need, or severe need child? Could we accommodate a wheelchair at our house? Would we house a child who had been sexually abused or one who was doing the abusing? Would we consider a child who was a fire starter? These were real questions. I was floored. Over twenty pages of these types of questions. What had we gotten ourselves into? I sat on our living room floor and cried. How could I help a child who had been through so much? We were not qualified to do this. My heart sank, and I started to pray. As I prayed, God reminded me that He does not call the qualified; He qualifies the called. I picked up my pen and completed the paperwork.

We soon found ourselves at the last class, anxiously awaiting to see if we had made the cut to become foster parents. By this time, our class had decreased in size by about ten. I am not sure why those who left chose to leave. Whatever the reason, I hope they found what they were looking for along their path. As for the rest of us, we sat in class waiting on our panel to get there. The panel contained former foster parents, a CPS worker, and a home finder, all ready to share their stories and experiences with us. They covered many of the basics, such as transportation and monthly stipend payments. They talked about the sorrow of seeing so many children in need and the joys of reunifying a family or helping a foster family become an adoptive family. Nevertheless, one thing was clear: they all loved doing what they did, regardless of how many times the system failed or the countless tears they had cried. They had made a difference, and that's what mattered most. They encouraged us, especially me. They helped spark a fire deep within me. I knew this was going to be hard. I knew there would be tears, there would be sorrow, there would be pain, but there would also be peace, love, and laughter. We were ready. We passed the class and would be opened for placement as soon as we received our certificate in the mail. Thank you, Jesus.

Waiting for the Call

> We know that all things work together for the good for those who love God, to those who are called according to his purpose.
> —Romans 8:28 (World English Bible)

We wrapped up classes in mid-November and were told that it could take up to six months before we got our first call for placement. After praying about things, at our home inspection we decided we could comfortably take on two children ages birth to five to start. Their race, gender, or disability did not make a difference. Now we just had to sit back and wait. We started what I called stockpiling supplies. We went to yard sales, thrift stores, and discount stores looking for affordable cribs, toddler beds, twin beds, mattresses, chests of drawers, toy boxes, toys, and even some basic clothes. Anything I thought a newborn up to a five-year-old might need I picked up. I had a room of totes full of things ready to go just in case we needed them. Every time the phone rang, I jumped. I would take my phone to the bathroom with me. I would take it with me to walk the dog and when I went to pick up my children from school. I knew the instructor said it would take months before we would get a call, but something inside me kept telling me to be ready. Then one day it happened.

It was late in November, barely two weeks after we finished our training. I was alone at the house. Our daughter and son were both at school, and my husband was at work. I had spent the morning washing up loads of clothes and was now relaxing on the couch watching some talk show on the television. My phone rang; I did not recognize the local number, but I answered anyway. Thinking it was a telemarketer, I said a quick hello. The voice on the other end sounded kind, but I could tell she was in a hurry. I honestly do not remember her name or the small talk at the beginning of the conversation. All I remember from that call is the following questions that came after all the introductions were over: "So I see you are an active foster family and that you have an opening. Is this correct?" I answered yes. "Good. Would you be interested in a baby boy around four months old for placement?" Again, I answered yes. "Great. I will call the caseworker back and let her know you are willing to take him."

I then found my voice and said, "But we haven't received our certificate stating we are open yet. We only finished training two weeks ago."

She laughed sweetly and said, "It's okay. You are on our list, so you check out. Welcome to the world of foster care." And just like that, we had a baby on the way.

The next few hours were a blur. I called my husband and told him. I sent text messages to our kids, and I called my mom, Todd's mom, and some close friends from church. And we waited. About six hours after I had taken the call, a small four-door car pulled into our driveway. I was a nervous wreck, full of mixed emotions. Two females stepped out of the car, both smiling and asking if they were in the right place. One looked like she had done this type of thing a time or two. In one hand, she held all the paperwork and a small plastic bag that contained a bottle, three diapers, one outfit, and a dish towel that was being used as a blanket. The younger lady seemed a little more like me. She had tears in her eyes as she handed the dirty car seat over to me. She said she had just fed him and that he needed a bath. I gathered him into my arms, and the four of us went into the house. We sat in the living room and talked about what they knew, which was not much. They gave me the paperwork that contained his medical card and his clothing voucher. I was told to take the voucher to Walmart and pick up whatever I needed for him, such as diapers, a diaper bag, wipes, and clothing. I also needed to buy him a new car seat. I was also given the name of his pediatrician and told to call and make an appointment for the next day. They wished us luck, and with that, they were gone. Here I sat with a new little baby boy who was scared to death, shaking, and dirty. I did not know what to do. So, we sat. I rocked him to calm him down. I sang him songs that used to quiet my children down, and he eventually drifted off to sleep in my arms. As he slept, I promised him we would get through this together. I thanked God for trusting us with this precious little boy. I prayed for His wisdom, His strength, and for His guidance. We were all in this together now, and I needed God's grace to get us through.

After he woke up, I gave him a bath, and we loaded up the van to go to Walmart. With him in one shopping cart and my husband pushing another, we headed to the baby section. We had three hundred dollars (we could spend less, but the voucher was only good for one shopping trip, so we had to shop wisely). The caseworker had told us to spend as close to three hundred as possible without going over. With that in mind off we went. I had made a list of things we would need: diapers, baby wipes, baby shampoo, bibs, a new car seat, socks, a coat, and some clothes. With my calculator in one hand and my list in the other, we set out on what would be the longest two-hour trip in Walmart history. We searched sizes and brands on everything from diapers to pacifiers. Things had changed a great deal since I bought stuff fifteen years ago for my little ones. Once the shopping cart was full, we headed to the service counter to check out. That's when I first noticed people looking at us, judging us. Many did not say a word; they just shook their heads, while others whispered, "Maybe I should quit my job and go on welfare. Look at all her 'free' stuff." While a few others said, "If you can't afford a child, why have one?" I was shocked. I found myself trying to explain the situation, that we were new foster parents and that he was our first placement and that I was sorry for taking up so much of the cashier's time. After all, I knew it was Christmas season and that the lines were forever long. That's when the subject changed to, "Why would someone not want that child? What's wrong with him for his parents to want to get rid of him?" Seriously? What's wrong with him? I could not believe my ears. How could anyone think that this sweet baby had done something bad? Why blame the child for something he clearly had no control over? Again, I was shocked. I went from apologizing for taking too long to full-blown momma-bear rage. I spoke my piece about how I thought they all needed to grow up, that it was not his fault his parents had made bad choices, and that if they were decent humans, they would stop judging the situation. I was mad, hurt, upset, and sad. How could adults judge this precious baby boy? I would like to report that this was a one-time situation and that everyone else I ran into along this foster care journey was more understanding. But that's not the case. It still happens today, all the time. The difference is I am now better at keeping my thoughts to myself instead of letting them pour out of my mouth.

    We made our way back home and unpacked the van. The next few days were taken up by doctors' appointments, people coming over to visit, and us adjusting to the newest temporary addition to our family. We even managed to attend a Christmas party with my parents and grandparents. He looked so sweet in his little Santa outfit. Life was great. About three weeks into our new adventure, I received a call from the caseworker's assistant. She asked if I had his stuff ready for her to pick him up. Pick him up? What was she talking about? I told her no and that I was not aware he had a visit with his birth mother that day. She apologized and said she assumed his worker had already called me. I of course said no and asked if something had happened. Apparently, there had been an emergency hearing for him the day before. He had a different last name than his siblings, so the connection was not made when he came into care. His three siblings were already in state care with an adoptable family. He was being moved to their home that day. I was devastated. She was sweet and sincere with her apology. She thought I knew. She gave me an hour to get his belongs together. An hour. That did not give my husband time to come home and say goodbye. That didn't give my kids the chance to say goodbye. I didn't have time to say goodbye because I was running around trying to get his stuff packed up. The worker and aide showed up right as our hour passed. Few words were exchanged. I kissed him on his forehead as they loaded him into the back of the car. As I turned to go back into the house, I heard the worker say, "I am so sorry."

With tears running down my face, I looked back and said, "It's okay. It's all part of foster care, right?" and I walked slowly back inside. Just as fast as he had come to us he was gone. The car pulled out of our driveway, and I watched until it was completely out of sight. I gathered myself together over the next two hours trying to figure out how I was going to explain this to my kids when I picked them up from school. When I pulled into the school parking lot I started to cry again. When Sierra and Devin got in the car and saw no car seat, they knew he was gone. I did not have to say a word. We all sat there in silence while tears fell to the floor. Their hearts were just as broken as mine. How could we do this again? We had only had him a few weeks, but he had our hearts. How could I put my kids and husband through this pain again? How could we continue? I did not know the answer; good thing God knew.

Beautiful Chaos

The Girls

Sugar and spice and everything nice that's what little girls are made of, Sunshine and rainbows and ribbons for hair bows that's what little girls are made of, Tea parties, laces and baby doll faces that's what little girls are made of.
—Unknown

After baby boy moved on to his new forever home, our hearts were heavy, and we felt lost. We prayed about which way to go, and after a few days, I made the call to the DHHR office to have them reopen us for placement. The lady who answered the phone checked our file and said she would be happy to pass our information along to the on-call home finder. We began the wait process again. No calls are good from a caseworker's point of view. No calls into the department to remove a child means we (the foster homes) are not needed. So, the days of waiting turned into a week. Weeks turned into a month. One month was quickly turning into two. Then it happened. We received a call for two little girls. One was getting ready to turn a year old, and the youngest was just a few months old. If we agreed to take them, we would pick up the youngest sister later that day but would have to wait a few weeks to pick up the oldest little girl. She was in the hospital. She had sustained injuries that required brain surgery. I called my husband and asked what he thought. His answer was, "Go with your gut. I trust you." I quickly called the worker back, and we accepted the placement.

The caseworker came to the house later that afternoon and handed me the smallest baby I believe I have ever laid eyes on. She could fit in the palms of my hands. Overall, she looked to be healthy and very alert. She was just so tiny and fragile. The worker told us the reason the girls had been removed and stated that visitations with the birth parents would most likely not happen for a while, if at all. This meant they would be a long-term placement. She handed us the girls' medical cards and vouchers for clothing and told us she would let me know when we could go to the hospital to pick up the oldest little one. With that, she got in her car and drove off. I pulled out her paperwork to locate her name and birthdate. I started making calls to get her in with a pediatrician and to get an appointment with the WIC office. She slept peacefully until it was time to go pick up the kids from school. They were a little surprised when I introduced them to our newest little one. The next few weeks were spent getting adjusted to having a baby in the house again and preparing for the arrival of her sister. God had seen fit to use us again.

We soon received the call that the oldest baby girl was ready to come home and that I could come to the hospital to pick her up. The caseworker provided me with the necessary paperwork stating that my husband and I were now her legal guardians, so I could get into the hospital. I walked in the hospital and made my way up to the pediatric floor. I stopped at the nurse's desk and told them who I was and showed them my paperwork. The charge nurse smiled and explained to me what surgery had taken place and why it had been necessary. My heart was breaking for this precious little one who I had not yet laid eyes on. The nurse started preparing me for what baby girl would look like with all the bandages and scars she would have due to the surgery. The nurse then told me that she had been alone most of her stay at the hospital. They, the staff, had taken turns going in to rock her and feed her, but they could not be with her all the time. The nurse's face turned sad as she told me that baby girl had not smiled or tried to get out of bed since coming out of surgery. I knew I had to get to her. I had to let her know that I was here now and that everything would be all right.

I walked into her private room, expecting to see a shell of a child. Lifeless and frail. What I got was the exact opposite. I peeked my head through the door and called out her name. Her eyes looked around to find my voice, and then our eyes met. For the first time in weeks, she wiggled her little body up to stand and reach out. She wanted me to pick her up. The nurse was blown away. She asked me if I was related to her or if I knew her, and when I replied no, she could not believe it. She quickly went out to the front desk to let her fellow nurses know that baby girl not only smiled but that she had stood up in her bed. I ran over and carefully picked her up, and she hugged me so tight. It was as if God told her she was safe now and that everything would be all right. I stood there just holding her for over twenty minutes, letting her feel safe and loved. We gathered her things she had in the room: a T-shirt that was too small for her, a teddy bear she had received from the surgery staff, a couple of diapers, and her discharge papers. Then we headed home. She smiled the whole way to the house. That weekend, we celebrated. We celebrated her making it through brain surgery. We celebrated her coming home, and we celebrated her first birthday, complete with a party at our house that included cake, balloons, and presents. Lots and lots of presents.

We soon got in the routine of doctor appointments and visits from the caseworker. The girls settled in and quickly became part of our family. They were given cute nicknames, something we would do for all our foster children over the coming years. Many of our foster children have enjoyed picking their own nicknames out. We decided early on not to use any of their real names while in public. The nicknames were a fun way to keep their identities private. It would be safer for them and us while we were out and about in case we ran into unfamiliar or unknown family members. Even my older kids loved having code names, as they called it.

At one of the early visits from the CPS worker, we were told that both girls were born with a condition that caused deafness (Waardenburg syndrome) and that they were sure the youngest girl was deaf (at least according to the birth parents) and that the oldest girl had at least some hearing loss in one ear. The baby was so small we had not noticed any signs, and with the older one having brain surgery, we didn't think much about her not always answering us. It was time to call in someone who could help us. Thanks to a group called Birth to Three, we located an ASL (American sign language) teacher. She was from Ohio but made the weekly trip to our house to work with the girls and me, teaching us sign language. My son and daughter were a huge help. It was a learning experience for us all. The teacher would work with the girls and me during the day, and during the evenings, we would sit down and work on the unfamiliar words together as a family. We bought some signing videos, and we started off on the new path of communication with the girls.

The oldest little girl was healing nicely from surgery and had settled in being the baby sister to our older kids. The youngest little girl was a wonderful baby. They both were so loving and sweet. They won over our hearts immediately, as well as the hearts of all our friends and family. We took family trips to Tennessee and around the different parks in the state. Court dates and MDT meetings came and went, and all signs were pointing toward the girls being adopted out and not reunifying with their birth parents. If that were to happen, my husband and I had decided that they would stay with us; no need for the worker to look for another family to adopt them. They were home. They were ours.

Then one day in mid-May, we received a call from the girl's GAL (guardian ad litem/lawyer). She said she would be out to see us and let us know how things were going with the case. We were excited; maybe the girls were finally coming up for adoption. A few days later, the lawyer and a few other people familiar with the case came to our house. My husband had taken off work early, so he could hear the good news firsthand. We sat on our couch while the lawyer started explaining to us what was going on. The parental rights of both mom and dad had been terminated. That meant the girls would be going up for adoption, just like we had hoped. Our hearts were beating out of our chest with joy. Our dreams were coming true. But neither my husband nor I were prepared for what came next. The department had found a family member (an aunt) out of state who was willing to take the girls and raise them as her own. My mind could not comprehend what the lawyer was saying. Why had this aunt not stepped up before now? And where had she been for the past six months? They were our girls. Selfish thoughts perhaps but still my thoughts at the time. This was not the big news we wanted to hear. The lawyer said the family would have to pass a home inspection and go through a background check just like we did before any final decision was made. We would be given a chance to plead our case, and we would have to prove to everyone the girls were better off with us. Then the lawyer said the judge had ordered a visit for the newly found aunt and her family to meet the girls, which would happen within the next couple of weeks, and she would let me know when that was to take place. I looked at my husband and thought to myself, *This can't be happening again.* We sat there in complete silence as she continued about how this could be a good thing.

The next couple of weeks were spent going through our daily routine while preparing for the upcoming visit and working on what we would say to the judge and the panel when we got our chance. The worker called, and we set up a visitation at the local park. I was a nervous wreck, and so was my husband. We drove to the park and waited for the worker who was supervising the visit to call and give us an exact location for the meeting. After about half an hour, the aunt called and asked where we were. I told her we were at the park waiting on the worker to call us and give us the "good to go" and where to go for the visit. She was not happy we had kept them waiting, so I tried to explain the protocol. She did not really seem to care about the do's and don'ts. I could tell she was upset. I would have been, I'm sure. A few minutes later, the worker called me. He was not the girls' normal worker; he was just filling in for the weekend. He was also new and did not know he was supposed to call me. We drove over to the picnic area and for the first time laid eyes on the couple wanting to take the girls away from us. I explained that we were not trying to upset anyone, that we were just doing what the department had told us to do. There were no hard feelings, and the worker agreed to stay longer to make up for the time lost during the confusion.

I am not going to lie; I did not want to like them, and truth be told, I am sure they did not want to like us. The problem was they were genuinely nice and kind people with very similar backgrounds to ours. Both her husband and mine had been in the military. We both had children in the band, we both were active in church, the list of similarities went on and on. The aunt explained to me that she did not know that the girls even existed until the department called her. She was shocked when she found out she had two nieces in state care. Come to find out the girls had two more siblings that had been adopted out by an uncle, this lady's brother. When the department called him to see if he could take the girls, he declined. He simply felt he and his wife could not handle two more babies. He told the department about his sister and her family and asked the department to call her—maybe she could help. My heart hurt for her as I watched her tell me the story of what had happened to the girls' grandmother, her sister, and what was going on now with the family. She held the youngest little girl and smiled down at her while she laughed at the nickname we had given her. I could tell she too was already in love with her and her sister.

Over the next two hours, we enjoyed our picnic and our visit. We said our goodbyes and went home to await what was to happen next. The aunt and uncle traveled back to West Virginia a few more times for visits, and everything seemed to be going well. Before we knew it, time had come to have our voices heard at a hearing at the DHHR. We pulled in and were told to have a set in the waiting area. We were surprised to see the aunt and uncle there as well. They had also been called in to state why the girls should live with them. The whole situation seemed unsettling and nerve-racking. We were finally called back into the room, where a small group of people waited to hear our side. I provided pictures and stories of all the girls most important times up until that point. We talked about the trips we took, the love we shared, the bond we had with them, and the progress they had made while in our home. We poured our hearts out, fighting back tears with every word that came out of our mouths. The panel thanked us and told us they would let the judge know their decision. We had done everything we could do; it was in God's hands now. We walked out and nodded at the aunt and uncle, and we went on our way. Our phone rang a few days later, and we were given a court date a few weeks out. We were told to be there at 10:00 a.m.

Our life was complete chaos. We did not know what was going to happen with the girls' case. I felt helpless. A few months before we received the news about there being a possible family match for the girls, my husband and I had planned a little weekend trip. With everything going on with the girls' case, we thought about canceling it. Looking back, I know God knew we would need this trip. It was part of His bigger plan. Sometimes He steps in, and we don't even realize it's Him. After debating about going or not going, we decided we needed to take a minute for us. We needed to reconnect with each other, the stress for the case was overwhelming. So, in the middle of all that was going on, my husband and I took our trip to clear our minds and calm our hearts. We made arrangements for the girls and for our older children and set out on our motorcycle. Our destination was a ski resort about three hours from our home. We arrived at our hotel and settled in for what we hoped to be a relaxing weekend. We enjoyed a peaceful dinner, took a romantic stroll around the resort, did a little shopping, and listened to a local music group perform outside one of the shops. Just what we needed.

Early the next morning, my phone rang while Todd was in the

shower. I was still half-asleep, so I did not answer it. A few minutes later, it rang again. Fearing one of the kids could be sick, I made my way over to the desk where my phone was charging and managed to get out a weak hello. The voice on the other end was one I did not recognize. I looked at the number on the caller ID and realized it was someone from the department. The sweet older voice on the other end told me she was the on-call worker for the weekend and that she had a baby boy who needed a place to stay until Monday—that's when his grandmother would pick him up. By this time, my husband was out of the shower and figured out what was going on by my side of the conversation. I told the worker we currently had a placement of two little girls and that in order for us to take the baby boy, we would have to get a waiver. She said getting a waiver would not be a problem seeing that he would only be with us for the weekend. I looked back over at my husband, who had already started packing up our clothes into the duffel bag. He is so great like that. He gave me the *Go ahead and tell her yes* look as he walked out the door to check us out of the hotel early. We agreed to take him but told her it would take a couple of hours for us to get back home. She said great, just to call her when we got back to the house. And just like that, our getaway turned into a get-a-new-baby day. We jumped on the motorcycle and headed back home.

A few weeks after Wild Man was placed with us, we had our court date for the girls. We arrived at the courthouse early, around 9:15, and were surprised that the hearing had already taken place.

We ran into the aunt, uncle, and the girls' GAL in the hallway and were told that the judge ordered that the girls be immediately placed with the aunt and uncle and that we had an hour to go pick up the girls and their belongings and be back at the DHHR building so that they could head back to their new home. Talk about a smack in the face. What happened to our 10:00 a.m. hearing? How could they change the time without telling us? Did us not being there affect the judge's decision? We thought we were going in and hopefully getting the "okay, you can adopt the girls," and the exact opposite happened. We were losing them forever.

We hurried home and gave a quick explanation to Todd's parents (they were watching the girls for us so we could go to court). For a few minutes, we just held the girls and cried. His parents gave the girls kisses and watched them as we packed up as much of their belonging as we could in the brief time frame. We loaded up the van and drove to the fast-food restaurant our daughter was working at so she could say a quick goodbye. We only stopped because it was on the way to the DHHR. I called my parents, but they did not get to say goodbye; we didn't have time to see them. I am so thankful they had seen the girls the night before while we were at our church for revival. My heart sank as we pulled in the parking lot. There, waiting by the back door, was the vehicle that would take the girls away from us forever. The aunt and uncle walked over and thanked us for taking good care of them. Their daughter gave me a note that thanked us as well (she was about seven at the time—I still have her precious note tucked away with some of the girls' photos). I gave them our home phone number and email addresses, so they could stay in touch if they wanted to, and told them when the girls would need to eat again. I hugged both girls one last time, kissed them on their foreheads, and whispered, "I love you forever" and "God, please be with her. Keep her safe in Your arms," in their ears. With tears running down my face, I got back in the car and held tightly to my husband's hand. Nine months had passed by from the time we first held them in our arms. We had watched them grow, gone on vacations, and taken them to church. We had loved them and made them part of our family in every possible way. And in less than two hours, they were taken away. As we pulled out, I could see the girls and their new family as they adjusted their seat belts getting ready to head off on their new adventure. I came home, picked Wild Man up, and held him tighter than I ever had. *God placed this little guy with us to get us through this heartache*, I thought to myself.

The aunt sent me a text after they arrived safely to their house. I thanked her, and with that, I was sure I would never hear from her again. The girls were now in their forever home. Time to focus on our Wild Man.

Wild Man and Little Miss

> They may not have my eyes, they may not have
> my smile, but they have all of my heart.
> —Unknown

Many times, in foster care, cases/placements overlap, as was the case for the girls and Wild Man. I mentioned earlier my husband and I were on a trip when we received the call asking us to take Wild Man in for the weekend. We checked out of our hotel early and drove straight home. I called the worker as soon as we walked through the door. She said she was still on call; however, she had already sent two of her coworkers out to drop the baby off to me. They were about fifteen minutes away from my house. We changed clothes and waited for them to arrive. The car pulled in our driveway as I was making coffee. The driver got out of the car first. He looked more like a cop than a CPS worker. He was tall with big muscles and had a serious look on his face. I thought to myself, *I see why the department would send him out to do a removal*. He was intimidating, very intimidating. As he walked toward me carrying the car seat, his serious look turned into a smile. He was super nice and told us he had enjoyed spending the morning with the little guy. The woman was fair skinned with long hair and had a warm smile. We talked out by the garage as she unpacked his things from the car. The woman worker said, "He is weak, but checked out okay at the hospital. Poor little guy. I hope he makes it through the weekend without ending up back in there." Taken by what she had said, I looked down to what was the second smallest baby I had ever seen. He weighed in at four pounds five ounces at two months old. The woman worker said they were told grandma would be picking him up sometime Monday and that one of them would call and let me know before they came out to pick him up. I assumed that grandma was out of town or maybe she needed time to get a room ready for him. Either way, he was here now, and he was safe until she could take him in. I thanked them, and we took him inside. He was so frail, so sick, so weak. I picked him up out of his car seat, and that's when I noticed the bedbugs he had been sitting in. I quickly threw the seat outside and called the worker to let her know. I didn't want them to get in her car. She of course thanked me and said she had not seen any bugs when they placed him in the seat. She asked that I take pictures and send them to her. So, I did right before washing the seat with bleach. The back of the car seat cover was covered in dead bedbugs. I can only assume the car ride had awaken the bugs, and some managed to crawl their way around to the front of the seat. My stomach turned. What had this poor baby been through in his short life?

Monday came and went with no word from his grandmother. We had him two weeks before our first big medical scare happened. It was the same day we were told he would finally be transferred to his grandmother's. He had been sick from the moment they placed him in my arms, but Wild Man took a turn for the worse that morning and quit breathing. I rushed him to the hospital and called the hotline for the on-call worker; that number was programmed in my phone, and his new worker's number was not. I explained to the on-call worker what was going on. I also told her that we had been notified his grandmother would be picking him up sometime that day, but that would not be possible, seeing that he was fighting to breathe at the hospital. The worker told me not to worry; she would track down his worker and let her know what was going on. My job right now was to care for him. She would handle the rest. My phone rang about twenty minutes later, and it was his worker. She asked for an update on Wild Man and then told me she had some news she needed to share with me. She had been contacted by the grandmother earlier that morning, and the conversation did not go as the department had planned. The grandmother had decided not to take him in. It was not because she did not love him; rather, she knew he was going to be a child with many medical problems, and she was not physically able to care for him. The worker then went on to tell me that if we did not want to continue to foster him, she understood and would find someone else after he made it out of the hospital. I looked over at the sweet baby boy, fighting so hard to breathe, fighting so hard to live. What if he didn't make it out? I told her that he was not going anywhere; he was to stay with us when he was discharged from the hospital. I called my husband and said, "Congratulations. It's a boy."

He did make it out of the hospital, within just a few short days—much earlier than any of the ER doctors had anticipated. His recovery demonstrated what the power of prayer can do. His caseworker came out to the house a few days later and could not believe how much better he looked. She had a small file with her that contained his background information—well, as much as we were entitled to have anyway, according to the State Department. Wild Man was born around thirty-one weeks, so he was considered a preemie. He was born drug dependent with two confirmed drugs in his system. According to reports, his mother also smoked cigarettes and drank alcohol on numerous occasions while pregnant. At one of the early court hearings, his mom stated she did not want him after finding out he was a boy so she "tried to self-abort him by taking whatever she could find." He spent three weeks on the NICU floor at the hospital before being released, a relatively brief time considering how long many drug babies and preemies must stay. I was in tears. He had been fighting for his life from day one. After being discharged, he and his mom made one of the shelters downtown their new home. According to the report, though I will never know the full details, his mom and dad began arguing one night, and it quickly escalated. His dad stormed off and left the shelter. His mom was overheard threatening to blow the baby's head off because it was his fault the dad was mad. She picked him up, shook him, then threw him across the room. His little frail body bounced off the wall and landed on a mattress. Someone walking by heard the commotion and ran into the room to see what was going on as his mom ran out the other door. He was taken to the hospital for treatment and observation. God had protected him through the ordeal. He had no broken bones, no internal bleeding, nothing. He was treated and after a few days released to us. We knew he had been mistreated but had no idea how bad. I vowed that day he would always know he was loved and know how special he was every day of his life. And to this day, I have kept my promise.

He had a rough first year. He had severe GERD (gastroesophageal reflux disease) and would throw up thirty to forty times a day. We had little pads, like the ones you use to house-train a dog, lying all over our house. He could be sitting on your lap or laying in the floor and out of nowhere projectile vomit across the room. It was like scenes from a scary movie. He also suffered from chronic ear infections, which lead to numerous hospital stays along with his acid reflux and stomach issues. He had several specialists we saw on a weekly basis: an ENT, a pulmonologist, his pediatrician, a hearing specialist, Birth to Three specialists, and a dietitian. He needed surgery to stop the vomiting, but he had to weigh fifteen pounds in order to have the surgery performed. Nothing we tried could keep his formula down. His doctor changed his formula multiple times and added rice to his bottles, hoping that something would work, but he still could not hold it down. His team of doctors decided to place him on steroids to help him gain the weight needed so he could move forward with the surgeries. In October, he finally hit the fifteen-pound mark, and we were given the green light for his first surgery. Within twenty-four hours, we were in Pittsburgh at one of the children's hospitals preparing for his procedures. He ended up with a G-tube placement for feedings and a Nissen fundoplication, also known as a laparoscopic fundoplication. The Nissen is a procedure in which part of the stomach is wrapped around the esophagus and stitched in place so that vomiting cannot take place. We made a total of five trips to Pittsburgh to have him treated over the next eight months. Doctors in Pittsburgh and doctors back at home told us they did not know what type or how active of a life he would lead because of his stomach issues or what long-term damage he suffered from being thrown across the room. It would be a wait-and-see game. At the time, we were happy knowing that he was no longer in pain from the excessive vomiting, and he would now be able to gain weight thanks to the feeding tube. We didn't have the answers but knew God had big plans for this special little guy and our family.

Wild Man was in the hospital for stomach issues when we were introduced, accidentally, to his half sister. I was sitting in the rocking chair holding on to my little guy when I noticed a lady walk into the room across the hall. I knew who she was when I heard her laugh; it was Wild Man's mom. I called the nurse to our room to see what was going on. I knew that his mom was not permitted to see him outside of their supervised visits. I also knew the nurses could not tell me why she was there, but they could keep her away from our room. I explained that I had seen his mom outside our room and that she was not permitted to have contact with him. The nurse informed me she was not there to see Wild Man. She was visiting the little girl across the hall. As we were talking, I heard his mom yell back into the other room, "Mommy will be right back." Mommy? She had another child? I didn't know she had another child. I had the nurse remove Wild Man's name from our door, and I pulled the door closed so that no one could see in. The staff promised to keep his stay there confidential, and they would let the social worker know about the situation. Talk about coincidence. How could both of her kids be in the hospital at the same time across the hall from each other?

That was the only day I saw her at the hospital. The next few days, the little girl had a man come and visit her. I assumed it to be her dad. No one ever stayed long, just short stops in and out to check on her progress. She was alone in her room most of the time for the next three days. My heart broke for her, but there was nothing I could do.

The day Wild Man was discharged, I heard people arguing in the hallway. The man was throwing a fit about taking his daughter home. The nurse came into our room and closed the door so we could not hear the angry words being exchanged. She finished up our paperwork and told me we were good to go. I asked if everything was okay but was told, "I'm sure it will be fine. We can't discuss other patients with patients." The nurse walked us to the front of the hospital, and we loaded up in the car and went home. All the way home, I wondered what was happening with that sweet little girl. I knew it was out of my control and that I had other things to focus on, like getting Wild Man home so we could prepare to go back to Pittsburgh. However, with God, nothing happens by coincidence; it's all part of His plan.

A few days after he was discharged from the hospital, we received a phone call about a placement. The worker had a little girl about sixteen months old that needed a temporary home. She knew we had Wild Man, and that's why she called us; this little girl was his half sister. The worker said she had been in the hospital recently but was doing okay. Of course, we said yes to the placement. This was the little girl who I had sat across the hallway from for close to a week, the same little girl I heard cry herself to sleep because no one was there to hold her, the little girl I heard the dad arguing over the day before. That little girl needed a home. The worker said she would be out shortly with her, so I started getting her room ready. I believe there was a reason she was placed in the hospital room across from us the week before. She and Wild Man had never met before, but as soon as she saw him, she crawled over and kissed him.

The police had gone to the father's home to execute a search warrant. They were told that the guy in question, aka her dad, had left early that morning with the little girl. The owner of the house let the cops search the house from top to bottom and the dad was not found. One officer, however, felt the need to search the playpen. According to what was reported, the officer said it was as if someone was telling him to look again in the playpen. The playpen was full of old pizza boxes, soda bottles, clothes, and trash. He used his nightstick to move the trash around so he could see down inside. He moved some of the dirty clothes, and there she was, sound asleep from an overdose of Benadryl. The officer picked her up and carried her out. The lady at the house was heard yelling, "He told me he was taking her with him! He told me he was taking her!" No one really knows how long she was there or what would have happened if the officer hadn't listened to the inner voice that told him to look again. She was taken to the ER and checked out, then brought to us.

When she arrived at our home, she was in a T-shirt that was two sizes too small and a pair of pants with a broken zipper. Her hair was a dirty brown color, and she smelled of cigarette smoke. The worker stated she had been in the hospital and treated for asthma several times, but the last hospital stay from a week earlier was to remove roaches from her ear. She was a mess. How could a baby have roaches in her ear? She needed a bath but was not happy about it. To tell the truth, I'm not sure she had ever had a real bath before; she screamed and cried, kicked her feet, and threw her head against the tub. When we washed her hair, we noticed it was not brown at all; in fact it was blonde. Yes, blonde. I called the worker and told her that after washing Little Miss's hair, we discovered her true hair color. I had to take a picture and send it to her to show her; she could not believe it. This poor baby had been through the unthinkable, and she was barely over a year. My heart broke for her. We got her cleaned up and settled in. That night, she slept for fifteen hours straight. I think she knew she was safe with us, and she finally let herself rest.

Beautiful Chaos

Quickly the court dates and meetings started taking place for both of our new little ones. Their mom was given visits with both Wild Man and with Little Miss, at separate times of course. Wild Man's dad attended only a handful of visits. He wanted nothing to do with the mom or the baby, so not showing up ensured his rights would be terminated. Mom herself visited Wild Man less than ten times. She claimed he was to sick and wanted nothing to do with him. In the grand scheme of things, it was probably best for him that they didn't stick around. His medical issues made it hard to keep him healthy in those early days. His grandmother was given one visit with him, so she could see that he was being cared for and to tell him goodbye. I know the visit had to be hard on her, but she thanked me for taking him in and loving him. She explained that she felt too old to take on the responsibility of being his full-time mother and that she wanted to give him the best opportunity she could. She knew he needed around-the-clock care, and she had to work; there was simply no way she could care for him. She kissed him on the forehead and said, "Promise me you will love him as your own."

I answered, "We already do."

Little Miss was a different story. Her dad received two-hour weekly supervised visitations, and her mom received a separate two-hour-a-week supervised visit. The parents could not get along well enough to do visits together, so twice a week, I loaded up my van and drove into town and dropped her off. She hated going; as soon as she saw the church where the visits were held, she would start screaming. I talked to her Birth to Three worker, and she agreed to start doing her visits there at the church with the dad so that someone Little Miss trusted would be in there to comfort her. The gentleman doing the supervised visits was awesome at his job. He truly cared about the well-being of Little Miss. He always had Little Miss in his sight during the visits. He documented every little detail. The visits went on for ten long months before the state ordered DNA paternity testing to determine if he was in fact her father. The man who she had been taken away from, the man who had been at the hospital with her, the man she was having visitations with turned out not to be her dad. Everyone, including him, was in shock.

The department was granted a new court date, and visits with him were terminated. When asked who her father was, her mom could not come up with an answer. So, the state placed an ad in the paper for an unknown father. The ad ran for forty-five days in the newspaper, and after no one stepped forward claiming to be her biological father, the department went forward with plans to terminate the rights of the unknown dad. To this day, we have no idea who her biological father is. After months of waiting, the unknown dad in Little Miss's case and Wild Man's dad were scheduled to be terminated along with their mom. I sat in the hallway outside of the courtroom, as I had for every court hearing, and I waited. Waiting for news, any news. In our county, foster parents are not permitted inside the courtroom while the hearings are taking place. So, I waited. I knew that the worker would eventually find time to call me and let me know what happened, but I figured out early on that if I was there waiting in the hallway as they came out, I would get the information much quicker, and that day, I finally heard the words we had been longing to hear. "The rights to all biological parents have been terminated on both children. The birth parents do have the right to appeal; however, we can start the paperwork so we can move the children over to the adoption unit after the appeal time is up—that is, if your intent is to adopt."

I could not help but feel sorry for their mom as she walked out of the courtroom. But at the same time, I was overjoyed that we were closer to becoming their forever home. As she passed me, she looked over and said, "I messed up. Take care of them until I can get them back please." Her lawyer pulled her to the side and explained again what had just taken place. I could tell she was in denial or maybe shock. As she made her way to the elevator, her eyes met mine again, and unlike the exchange that had taken place just a few minutes prior, this time there was only hate and anger looking back at me. My heart still went out to her. The drugs and alcohol had changed the course of her life. Her children would have a chance at a good life now, but it would no longer be with her. The words "both Wild Man and Little Miss are free to be adopted" played over and over in my head. I quickly called my husband, my parents, and in-laws to let them in on the good news. We were through the hard part; the rest should be easy.

Moving Forward

> We keep moving forward, opening new doors
> and doing new things because we're curious and
> curiosity keeps leading us down new paths.
> —Walt Disney

We were going to be a forever family of six. It was time to celebrate. My mother, daughter, son, Wild Man, Little Miss, and I headed to Disney World to celebrate. It made perfect sense to celebrate the happy news at the happiest place on earth. We still needed permission from the department to take them out of state, but it was time to celebrate. We could wait a few days on the paperwork. After receiving the paperwork, we were on our way to see Mickey and his crew. We enjoyed the Magic Kingdom for a few days and even took a day to visit Sea World. Seeing the looks on my children's faces as we watched the parade and as we waited in line to get autographs was priceless. One of the other highlights of the trip was watching my mom meet Goofy for the first time. She loves Goofy. We were having a wonderful time staying up late, eating way too much theme park food, and enjoying all there was to see and do. However, by Thursday, Wild Man had started breathing oddly, and we decided to cut the vacation short and get him back home so his pediatrician could see what was going on with him. I called his doctor while we were traveling back and got him an appointment for the day we would arrive in town. The diagnosis: the change in the climate had affected his lungs, which was making it hard for him to breathe. On top of that, he had picked up a virus. I did not think going on vacation would lead to a hospital stay for him, but it did. We spent the next week not at Disney but on the pediatric floor at our hospital receiving around-the-clock care. Not exactly the type of room service we planned. His system was still so fragile. I felt awful for not knowing the climate change would affect him as much as it did. Lesson learned.

After his hospital stay, we started moving forward with the adoption. We worked on child summaries and all the other necessary paperwork. We continued the countless doctor appointments and Birth to Three visits to keep Wild Man on track. We also worked through the list of new possible names for our new little loves. Life was going great. Once the adoption was final, our house would be too small to take on any new placements, so we sold our house and bought a larger one in the same area. One evening while working on some of the seemingly endless paperwork, my husband and I discussed our future as foster parents. We talked about it, prayed about it, and decided that after we were completely moved into the new house, we would reopen for placement while we were waiting for the adoption to take place. A few weeks after we were all moved in, I called and reopened our home for placement. Later that same night, our phone rang, and it was a call for a sibling group, two little boys around the ages of five and three. After hearing what background the caseworker had on them, we agreed to take them in. So much for getting used to having an extra bedroom. We sat and laughed as we talked about how fast God was moving in our lives.

The boys came to us as a temporary placement. They had been in and out of foster care since the youngest was a baby. The information we received was that their fathers (same mother, different fathers) were in prison, and the mom had not been seen for some time. They had been bounced around from foster home to foster home. It was like a story plot from a television show. The foster families they had been with, unfortunately, were not much better than the home they had been removed from. By the time they arrived at our house, they were broken. The oldest had taken on the role as the protector. He was old enough to understand what was going on and felt he needed to keep his little brother safe. Just two days after his arrival, he was yelling and kicking at Wild Man, and when I told him to stop, his reply was, "I don't have to follow your rules. They are stupid. I don't like it here. All I have to do is act up until you hate me, and they will move us again." He was five. Five. He had been neglected and abused so much his answer to life was, if you don't like something just act out until they move you somewhere else. He had never experienced love, so there was no love in his heart or in his actions. He only knew that bad actions gave him attention. And he was starving for attention; it did not matter if it was good or bad.

However, as the weeks went by, we had some good days. When he wanted to be a good kid, he was a great kid. His circumstances had never given him a chance to be anything but troubled until coming to our home. After he warmed up to us, his temper calmed down, and he tried to make the most out of his stay. He had a smile that could melt your heart, and on days he liked you, he would give the biggest bear hugs. He longed to be loved, and that's what we gave him. As for his education, we enrolled him in his sixth kindergarten class within that year. He was so lost he barely knew his ABCs and trying to get him to focus on his work was challenging because he just did not care. The youngest little guy had some behavior problems of his own. He would hit and punch or scream to get attention. Again, all they knew was violence. They did not understand how to interact with others in a positive or nurturing way. They needed someone to show them how to interact with others, how to show love, and how to be loved. They needed someone to show them that they were good boys, that they were worth fighting for, and that nothing that had taken place was their fault. I could not help but think the system had let them down. Being in one bad foster home was hard enough; being in more than one was unacceptable. If they had been placed in a good home, a loving home to start out with, then maybe they would be less angry at the world.

Before we knew it, they had been with us for two months. We had come up with a new routine, and things were becoming more manageable with six kids. One of our biggest obstacles was the oldest boy would not listen to anything I had to say and seeing that I was with him more than my husband, it made things somewhat difficult. I questioned the caseworker as to why she thought we were having problems with him listening to me, and the answer was the typical. "He has been through so much, and he is old enough to understand what is going on. Just be patient with him." I understood that he had been though a lot, but how was I to help him if he would not listen to me? The only emotions he really understood were hate and anger. If I told him something he did not like, he would look at me with pure hatred in his eyes. He could be the sweetest boy, but when I would tell him it was time to do his homework, the fight was on. He would start yelling at me, telling me he hated me, hated my husband, and hated our kids and that he would make us pay. I knew he was just a little boy, but when he went into those raging meltdowns, he was capable of anything. He needed someone to help him work through his anger. In his eyes, everyone that he had loved or who had loved him was gone. He was in fight-or-flight mode constantly. He did not want to get close to anyone for fear of getting hurt again. It was hard to see him struggle, knowing that none of his actions were his fault. His past would not let him have a future.

Right before Easter, we had an incident take place at the house. I don't know what it was about this particular event, we had seen far worse, but this is the one that changed things. The fighting between the children had grown more intense over the last few months. I know kids will fight and argue, but it had become a constant at the house. Nothing we seemed to try made life peaceful. One evening I was in the kitchen making dinner when I heard Little Miss scream out in pain. I ran into the family room where the children had been playing. There I found the three-year-old boy holding Little Miss down as he went to punch her in the face. The oldest boy was sitting on Wild Man to hold him down. My soon-to-be daughter's eyes were already turning dark from where I could only assume by her scream she had already been hit at least once. My son came running down the stairs and saw me trying to pull the little guy off her. It took both of us to separate them. I had my son take the other children to the living room while I sat and held the out-of-control three-year-old. He kicked me, bit me, and screamed at me for what seemed like hours. His facial expressions were haunting. The fact that this had become a normal part of our routine left me feeling defeated. After a few hours, I finally got him calmed down. I was exhausted. We both were. I knew I could not handle them anymore. We were still in the adoption stage, so every incident and every injury had to be reported. I did not want the boys to move, but I knew when I made the call to the worker to give the report what would happen. After I made sure Little Miss had no other injuries and that Wild Man was okay, I pulled myself together and called the caseworker. I explained the situation and was told she thought it best if the boys were removed. The caseworker knew of all the other problems we were having with the boys and understood our concerns. With a heavy heart, I said, "Yes, I think it's best if you find them another home," when she asked. She said all right and agreed to look for another home to place them in.

A few days later, I took the boys to the grocery store with me. As we were checking out, an older woman yelled out the youngest boy's name and ran over to hug him. I quickly got in between the two of them and asked her who she was. I know that sounds mean, but I did not know who she was, and with them being in state care, I could not let them have contact with anyone other than those they had scheduled visits with, for their safety and ours. She told me that she was his grandmother and that she was fighting the system to get custody of him. She asked if I could let her see him. I told her that was not up to me. I suggested that if she really wanted visits with him, she should call the department and ask to speak with his caseworker; she would be the one to set visitations up. She gave me a dirty look but agreed to call the department to see if something could be arranged. She backed up but continued to talk to me. I placed my groceries on the counter with one hand so that the cashier could start checking them out, while I kept one arm around the boys. The grandmother was clearly upset that her grandson was in foster care, but I questioned, to myself, Why had she not stepped up to get custody of him earlier? After all, he had been in state care most of his young life. Where had she been? Why did the state not place him with her first? The state always looks for family members first for placement; it's easier on the children. These are all questions that run through a foster parent's mind when running into a foster child's biological family unexpectedly.

She must have seen that I had questions because she began to tell me her story. She told me that she had been trying to get her grandson placed with her since she heard he had been "taken by the state," but the state had not made it a straightforward process for her. They "wanted her to jump through hoops" to get him, and in her eyes, that was just not fair. She went on to thank me for taking him in. "I can't believe that another foster mom accused him of hitting her baby girl. He would never do such a thing," she said. I stopped and looked at her. I asked when she had received that information. She told me that she had been in contact with the caseworker and was informed that the boys were being moved again. She assumed that the move had taken place, seeing they were with me. I paused and told her that the boys had been with me for the last several months. That's when she realized I was the little girl's mom. She started questioning my parenting skills and asked why I had lied about her grandson. The cashier could tell the grandmother was getting upset and quickly loaded my groceries back into my shopping cart. As we walked out the door, she continued to scream at me. The boys held onto me tightly and got into the car without any complaints. They were terrified.

That evening was one of the most peaceful evenings we had at the house while they were with us. They were both so loving and warm. The oldest thanked me for keeping them safe. The youngest kept holding my hand. We did not shop at that grocery store again.

A few days later, their worker called and told me she had found a possible family for the boys and that the mom wanted to set up a playdate to get to know the boys. I agreed, and we exchanged information. She came out and picked up the boys a few days later. They spent the day with their possible new family getting to know them and them getting to know the boys. The couple had older children and a few grandchildren. When they came home, they were both smiling and seemed happy. That was a good sign. After discussing the plan with her husband, they agreed to become the boys' new foster family. We agreed that since the oldest boy had been in and out of so many kindergarten classes, they would take him to school in the mornings, and he would ride the bus to my house in the evenings and stay until she could get off work. That way, he would not have to transfer again. This would be the best solution for him. On the last visit from the caseworker, I ran the plans past her, and we finalized the move. She was grateful that their new foster mom and I were willing to work together to make the transition easier for the boys. As we talked, their worker brought up how the boys, especially the oldest, had been through so much with his mom and that she felt he had a lot of resentment he needed to work through. I asked about his biological mom and was given a vague background, and then she told me that I kind of looked like her. I had the same hair color, the same body frame, and even to a point sounded like her. That's when we both had that *now it makes sense* moment. "You really do look a lot like her. Maybe that was part of the problem." So, he didn't hate me? He defied me because all he saw when he looked at me was his mom. The mom who had left him, the one who talked down to him, the one he felt did not love him, the one who had given up on him. It would not have made a difference if I had given into everything he asked; in his eyes, I did not care. If only I had known that, maybe the last few months would not have been so hard on him. I can't imagine what he was going through every time he looked at me or heard my voice.

A few days later, it was time for them to move. We had all their belongings ready to go when their new foster mom arrived to pick them up. We talked for a few minutes as we loaded her car with all the boys' things and exchanged phone numbers and friendly hugs. I hugged both boys and told the oldest I would see him Monday after school. He smiled and said, "Have my chocolate milk ready please." I laughed and agreed to do just that. I waved goodbye as they drove off and went back into the house. The transition had gone smoother than either of us anticipated. I had a good feeling the boys would be just fine in their new home.

Two hours after they left, the phone rang. "I hear that you are open for placement," the voice on the other end stated.

I laughed and said, "Well, I guess I technically am. The boys have only been gone two hours."

The caseworker, the same worker who had called us about Wild Man, laughed and said, "When good foster homes become available, word travels fast."

She told me about two little girls she had on her caseload. They had spent over a year living with their aunt and uncle, but recently the uncle had passed away. The aunt had tried to care for the girls on her own, but due to her growing health problems, she could not continue. She needed to find the girls a new home. The case looked to be one that would lead to adoption, but it was still too early to say. I sat there for a few minutes and thought about what my husband would say and then answered, "Bring them to us." She said she would be at our house after work sometime around five thirty. I went upstairs and looked at what had been the boys room just a few hours before. I pulled the baseball sheets off the beds and replaced them with princess sheets. I straightened up the toy box and pulled out a few dolls and Barbies from storage. In less than twenty-four hours, we went from a family of six to a family of four back to a family of six. The life as a foster care parent is always changing.

The worker arrived with the girls right around five thirty. By this time, I was accustomed to the drop-off routine and knew what questions to ask and what questions would go unanswered. The girls held tightly to the worker as she discussed the case and what the plans were. I smiled at the oldest girl, and she replied with a nervous, halfhearted smile. The youngest, however, took a leap of faith and ran over and climbed on my lap. I gave her a hug, and she looked up at me and said, "I think I will like it here." The worker and I spent the next thirty minutes going over a beautiful handwritten letter the aunt had sent, consent forms to take the girls to a new pediatrician, and the clothing voucher. The worker picked up her purse, hugged the girls goodbye, and told them she would see them in a few weeks. I walked her to the door and waved as she drove out the driveway. I came back into the living room to find the girls and Little Miss already bonding over baby dolls.

The oldest girl was fair skinned, thin and had light, reddish-blonde, curly hair. She was on the quiet side and was cautious of her surroundings. The youngest one, around three and a half at the time, was the opposite. She had brown hair, straight as a stick, her skin was olive with freckles, and she looked healthier than her sister. She was full of smiles and giggles. Little Miss took right to her, and they instantly became best friends.

Beautiful Chaos

I pulled out their paperwork after they were in bed fast asleep and realized that the oldest one's birthday was in a few days. We were having Wild Man's birthday party the following day. I could not have a party for him knowing her birthday was coming up soon. I called my mom and asked her to come down and sit with the kids so my husband and I could run to the store to buy her a few gifts. We didn't know much about her, but being that she was turning five, we played it safe and bought Barbie dolls, a bouncy ball, and some clothes. The next morning as we sat up for the party, she told me that she thought she had a birthday coming up and that she was sad because she was no longer at her mom's house, so she would not be having a party. I smiled at her and asked her to follow me to the kitchen. I picked her up and told her to look at the birthday cake. She gave me a puzzled look but did as I asked, and when she saw her name on the cake, she squealed out in absolute joy. She was so excited. As our family arrived, they were greeted and introduced to our newest additions. We managed to pull off not only Wild Man's birthday but also her birthday, complete with cakes, presents, ice cream, and her favorite food, pepperoni pizza. To think, less than twenty-four hours before, we did not even know her. God is so good.

The next two months went by quickly. The girls loved going to church with us and singing along with the choir. They played well with Little Miss and enjoyed having their toenails and fingernails painted. They were definitely girly girls, and we loved it.

Our family's annual vacation with my parents to Gatlinburg was just around the corner. I had tried to change our reservations but was not having any luck finding a cabin to fit our needs on such a short notice. The problem was, counting the girls and my parents, we needed room for ten, but the cabin was zoned for eight. When the reservation was made, the girls were not with us. Vacation season was in full swing, and another cabin could not be found. I was devastated. Looking back, I know God's hand was at work, but at the time, all I could think about was not being able to take the girls with us. I broke down and called the girls' worker and told her what was going on. We would have to use the respite service. Respite is where another foster family will watch your foster child if you need to go out of town for work, if you need to go to the doctor, or if you are going on vacation. Each child in West Virginia foster care receives fourteen days of respite care a year if needed. In this case, we had to use respite care service. This was the first and only time up to date we have ever used it; we normally took our foster kids with us everywhere we went, including vacation. God had a plan. The worker said she would look around and see if anyone was open to watch the girls the week we were gone. I received a call back a few hours later and was told they had found a couple willing to take the girls in while we were gone. This couple, Jon and Nadine, were new to foster care. They had recently finished their classes and thought watching the girls for a week would be a wonderful way to introduce themselves to the world of foster care.

Upon talking with Nadine, we all agreed it would be nice for the girls to meet them before we dropped the girls off for a week, so we arranged to have lunch at a local fast-food place about a week before we were scheduled to leave. We pulled in and looked for their car. My husband and I got out of our car and were working on getting the girls out as Jon and Nadine approached our car. We all walked in the restaurant together and found a booth that had adequate seating for us all. There was a calmness that came over me as we talked. The girls ate their hamburgers and colored while the four of us adults got to know each other a little. They were a lot like my husband and myself. They were both active in their church, they were huge Green Bay Packer fans, and both had a passion for foster care. The youngest little girl quickly warmed up to Jon and went to sit on his lap while the oldest sat between me and Nadine. Our conversation was not like strangers at all, more like old high school buddies catching up. We all agreed that we would drop the girls back off the following week at this same spot. They were excited, and so were the girls. I was not happy about having to leave the girls behind, but God gave me peace in the fact that they seemed to be kind and loving people, and that made me happy.

The following week drew near, and I started telling the girls they would be going and staying with our new friends for a week. They were both excited to see Jon and Nadine again. As we pulled in, the girls started smiling. They both ran up to Jon and gave him a hug and then ran over to hug Nadine. We exchanged phone numbers, and I gave them the medical cards in case of an emergency. We kissed the girls goodbye and headed back to our house to pack up what we would need for vacation.

I sent Nadine a message when we arrived at the cabin to let her know the number of where we were staying. I told her to give the girls hugs and kisses for us and we went on with our evening plans. It felt odd not having the girls with us, but I knew they would have a fun time with all the things Nadine had planned. I called Nadine a few more times while we were gone just to check in and see how things were going. She always sounded so happy, and the girls were loving every minute of their stay. Our family took part in all touristy things to do in Gatlinburg, and our vacation time quickly came to an end. I called Nadine to let her know we would be heading back home and that we would be there to get the girls the next morning. That's when God intervened. She had a question to ask me, a big one, one that would change everything. She and Jon had been praying for years for God to bless them with children, and they had fallen in love with the girls. She was not sure how to say goodbye; she didn't want to. She and Jon had prayed and felt that God was calling them to take in the girls as their first foster placement. She asked me if the girls could just stay with them. I told her I could not make that call and did not know if that was even possible, but if they were sure that's what they wanted, I would talk to the girls' caseworker.

Now, before you get mad at me, let me explain. Todd and I had no intentions of adopting any more children after Little Miss and Wild Man were officially adopted. And if these girls were going to be adoptable, then why not go ahead and place them with a family wanting to do just that? Why make them wait for their forever family? So, I called their worker and asked her. The girls deserved their forever family. The worker agreed that if we did not plan on adopting the girls, it would be best for them to move in with Jon and Nadine. We had worked together enough that if I felt it was a good call, she trusted my judgment. I called Nadine back and told her that we were given the green light and that the girls could stay with them. I love how God works; it truly amazes me. We decided to meet up with them the following day so we could give the girls their things and tell the girls the good news. When we arrived and saw how happy the girls were, my heart melted. The youngest one told me all about the week she had; playing dress up, going to church, and going to the park were just a few of the highlights. The oldest girl was all smiles. Better than all smiles, she was happy, really happy. They were so excited to hear that they were getting to stay. We all hugged and promised to stay in touch. God used a crowded cabin to get the girls where they needed to be.

Beautiful Chaos

God Makes Us All Unique

> Autism: Where the "Randomness of life" collides and crashes with an individual's need for the sameness.
> —Eileen Miller

After the girls went to live with Nadine and Jon, we continued to move forward with the adoption of Little Miss and Wild Man. As Wild Man grew, we started to notice that he was not developing like other children his age. We were told with his background and all his surgeries, he would need extra time to catch up. But there was more to it than that. By the age of two, he was falling behind with many of the normal milestones. Family and friends told us not to worry, but we knew something was wrong. He was not saying many words, and he was still eating only baby foods. But the biggest obstacle was his sleeping, or should I say lack of sleeping. He would stay awake for days at a time; sleep was not something he did. He could go weeks on as little as four hours of sleep a day, and that included his naps. Every few weeks, he would crash and sleep for fourteen to sixteen hours straight. Whenever he woke up, be it seven in the morning, three in the afternoon, or midnight, that would reset his schedule, and we would start the next round of sleepless days and nights. His schedule was all mixed up. Something had to be done.

By that point, he had a large medical team working with him. We had his pediatrician, his surgeon, his speech therapist, his OT, all his

Birth to Three workers, his ENT, and even a dietitian. We modified everything we could, changed his eating habits, which was not easy with his sensory issues, and started him on Melatonin to help put him to sleep at night. The problem was, with him not getting enough sleep, his body and brain were not resting, so his system could not reboot. Without resetting or rebooting, his body did not know it needed sleep or understand he needed rest. See the problem? Without one, the other could not function properly; we had to figure out a way to get his sleep pattern, body, and mind all working together.

One of his Birth to Three workers thought he may have more than just sensory issues. She had seen similar sleep patterns in a few of her kid clients who were autistic. She thought we needed to discuss the possibility of him being on the autism spectrum with his pediatrician. I was not familiar with the autism spectrum, so I researched and discovered he did fit many of the things to look for. The diagnosis made sense. He would line his cars in straight lines all around the house. The cars always faced the same way and were always from smallest to largest. He would sit and spin for hours, he did not sleep, he was more for parallel play than actually playing with others, he could stack cars on top of each other fifteen to twenty high, and the few words he could say he would repeat in sets of three, such as "No, no, no" or "Dad, Dad, Dad." His team of doctors agreed, and when he turned three, we were referred to a psychologist to have testing done. Not knowing what to expect, I had my best friend go with me to our first appointment. Wild Man does not do well in new surroundings, so I wanted someone there to help calm him down if needed.

I'm glad she went with me because he was terrified when we stepped in the office. He went into full-blown meltdown mode. The doctor was kind and let him play with some toys while she asked me a few questions as we both tried to calm him down. When it was his turn to start taking the test, we ran into some difficulty. He became frustrated and distracted. What should have taken two hours turned into four hours. It was what I call a nightmare appointment. A few weeks went by, and the results were in. According to the results, he was on the autism spectrum. I took the results to his pediatrician and expressed my concerns. I knew he had not tested well because he was upset when we were there. So, we agreed to have a second opinion. I was not in denial that something was different about my son, but I had to be sure, and thankfully, his doctor agreed. The second psychologist appointment went much smoother. One of his Birth to Three workers went with me. She and I had become good friends by that point, and she would be able to answer some of the developmental questions better than I could. We took turns talking with the doctor, and then she performed his part of the test. This time, he struggled, but we managed to get out of the office without any major meltdowns.

Again, we waited, and within a few weeks, we had the results. Our three-year-old son was diagnosed with autism. I sat in my living room floor and cried. Was I upset? A little. Was I relieved? A little. I had a thousand thoughts and questions running through my mind. Could we handle this? Was this the result of his birth mother's bad choices? Could I have done something different that would have prevented this? I feared the unknown. I was scared for him and scared for us. I had heard of autism before but did not know anyone with it. What if we were not strong enough to handle what was to come? What if I was not strong enough? I did not know what to do. Now that we had a diagnosis, what happened next? He was now three, too old for future Birth to Three services but not old enough for preschool. He was stuck in the middle. His Birth to Three team stepped up to help us, even though he had aged out of their services. They were a fantastic group of ladies to work with, and they cared deeply about his future. Even though he was too old for them to work with, they helped me find other sources to accommodate what he needed. One of his Birth to Three workers even made him a weight blanket to help him with his sleeping issues. Wild Man still sleeps with that blanket every night. It has been a godsend. With their help, we found a therapy group that offered him speech, OT, and music therapy. We also were able to have him tested for preschool, and with his scores, he qualified for the county's special needs preschool program. We were finally on the right path.

God Had a Bigger Plan— Introducing Big Al and Elmo

God knew it doesn't matter how your children get to
your family. It just matters that they get there.
—Kira Mortenson

Wild Man and Little Miss had been in our care a little over two years when we received the call we had longed to hear. We had been given possible dates for the adoption to take place, but time after time the date changed. We were beginning to think it would never happen. One Saturday in early July 2013, my parents had come to the house to visit. I asked if they cared to watch the kids so that my husband and I could run to the store. As we drove to the grocery store, my phone rang. "We have an adoption date" is all I heard from the voice on the other end. "September 20, 2013, you will officially become the parents to Wild Man and Little Miss." I started screaming so loudly my husband thought something bad had happened. I quickly took down all the information and got off the phone.

When I told my husband what had happened, he stayed calm and said, "Well, all right, it's about time." As we talked about the details, we both looked at each other and said that our journey as foster parents would end after the adoption. The amount of time, energy, and heartache was just too much to continue. We went to the store and hurried home to share the news with everyone. We had a few months to plan the forever family party and could not wait to celebrate. We pulled out the tattered list of possible names and finally agreed on names for our soon-to-be new son and new daughter. Life was perfect.

That following Wednesday night while my husband was at church, my oldest daughter and I were home with the kids. My house phone rang—something always happens when my phone rings, if you haven't noticed by now—so I answered it. The lady on the other end asked if we still had an opening for a child. I told her we were in the process of adopting the two children in our care and after the adoption our plan was to close our home. She paused with, "Oh I'm sorry to hear that." She then explained she was trying to find a home for a baby boy. My mind went back to the conversation I had with my husband just a few days prior. With a heavy heart, I told her we could not take him in. She thanked me for my time, and I hung up. By this time in our foster parent journey, we had turned away over 150 children, but saying no was never easy for me. Many circumstances were sibling groups we simply did not have room for. A few we were not equipped to handle their medical needs. Every time I said no, I would get off the phone and say a prayer. I would ask God to protect the child/children, and I would ask Him to find them a safe and loving home. After spending a few minutes in prayer, I would then go on with my day. This night, however, after saying my prayer for this little boy, I could not get myself to move on. When my oldest daughter asked who was on the phone, I told her it was a worker that had a baby boy who needed a place to call home. I found myself in tears and could not help being worried about this little boy.

By the time my husband made it in from church, I was what my older kids call "a hot mess." My husband asked what was wrong, and I told him about the phone call I had received. He could clearly see I was upset and then spoke words I never thought I would hear him say. He held me in his arms and said, "Call the worker back and tell her if she's not found a placement for him, we will take him in. After all, what's one more?" I was in shock. Had he just said call her back? I looked at him and then looked at the clock. It was 10:30. I held his hand and told him it was too late to call her back. I convinced myself that since he was a baby, the worker would have no trouble finding him a home. However, I agreed to call the worker in the morning to check on him.

That night, I had one of the most amazing dreams I have ever had in my life. I dreamt of my grandfather. He had passed away over Thanksgiving the year before. In my dream, my grandfather told me how proud he was of me and how he was thankful Todd and I were doing God's work. Then he pulled me close and said, "Sweetie, that baby boy is meant to be yours. He is meant to be part of our family." When I woke up, I had this peace I cannot explain. I patiently waited till 8:30 before I called the on-call worker back. When I called, she did not answer, so I left a message asking her to call me back. I told her that my husband and I had talked about it and prayed about it, and if the baby boy was still without a home, to bring him to us. I knew the chances of her calling me back were slim to none. He was a baby, and babies always get placed quickly in foster care. This time, I hung up the phone and went on about my day. I had done everything in my power; whatever happened next was not up to me. Thursday evening came, and no phone call back from the worker. When my husband came home from work, I told him I had called the worker and left a message but had not heard back from her. We both assumed the worker had found a place for him to call home, and we were okay with that.

The next morning, I got up and helped my husband and oldest daughter get ready for their annual motorcycle ride to Washington, DC. It would be just me and three kids for the weekend. God, however, had another plan. That afternoon, my phone rang. It was the on-call worker. She apologized for not calling me back, the week had been unfortunately full of removals, and asked me if we were still willing to take the baby boy in. I was floored. I quickly said yes, and she said, "Great. See you in a few hours. I will explain everything then." I spent the next few hours preparing the nursery for our new little guest. I had assumed that the baby would be around six months old. Normally, when previous workers had used the term "baby," they meant in the six- to nine-month age range. When she arrived, however, she had a beautiful three-day-old baby boy in her arms. My heart melted. His hair was dark and wavy, his eyes a deep brown, and his complexion was perfect. The worker told me that the birth mom had decided to place him up for adoption. She, his mother, had other children that she did not have in her custody and knew she could not care for him and there was a couple that planned on adopting him. However, when they arrived at the hospital shortly after he was born, they stated that "he was too black for their family" and decided against taking him home. So, he was placed in state care. His mother was biracial; they knew that. I'm not sure what the couple was expecting. Too black? Seriously? How could anyone say that? I was furious. He was gorgeous. They had made a horrible judgment call, and we would receive the gift of this little boy. He was the picture-perfect baby.

I was told he had some drugs in his system, marijuana and benzos, and that I would have to set up an appointment with a pediatric cardiologist and neurologist to have him evaluated. We talked for a few more minutes before her phone rang about another possible removal. We scheduled a follow-up visit for the following month, and she drove away. I took a picture of him and sent a text message to my husband and daughter saying, "Surprise! It's a boy!" I would have loved to have seen the look on their faces when they received it.

When my husband and daughter arrived home the following Monday, our house was full of active little ones. I had already scheduled our new little guy's, now known as Big Al, doctor appointments and made plans for Birth to Three to come out and evaluate him. Our pediatrician was happy to take him on as a new patient, and the specialists agreed to work him in as quickly as they could. His first few weeks at our house were challenging. He would wake up around two every night and would not go back to sleep. In talking with some of my foster parent support group friends, we decided he was still going through some withdrawal from the drugs in his system. Not sure if that was the case, but this pattern did last about eight weeks before he could wake up and then go back to sleep. Overall, he was the perfect baby. He was happy, he was alert, he ate well, and he had the happiest laugh.

A few weeks into his stay with us, the caseworker called and told me she was still looking for a forever home for him but was not having much luck. I told her it was fine, we did not mind having him around. I could not believe they were having problems finding a home for him, but my mind kept taking me back to the dream of my grandfather. I questioned myself. Could it be? Was he really meant to be part of our forever family? The worker came out later that month for our monthly visit and was pleased to see him doing so well. I told her about him not sleeping, but all in all, that was the only thing I could think of to warn his potential new parents about. She told me she would continue the search and that if she found a suitable fit, she would let me know. My heart told me she would not find anyone; he was where he was meant to be. I just needed to figure out a way to tell my husband. So, that evening after dinner, I asked him if we could talk. I think he knew what I was going to say before I even said it. I gave him my reasons for why I thought Big Al needed to stay with us and stated that the department was having a tough time finding him a forever home. I was ready to hear, "Now, honey, we already discussed this and agreed to stop after the adoption speech," but instead he said, "Okay, if you really feel he is meant to be ours, then he is. We will become a family of seven." I truly have an amazing husband. His heart is so big, and he understands me more than anyone else. I am blessed God placed him in my life.

I called the worker the next day and told her to stop looking for a home for Big Al, that we had decided he was meant to be with us. She was so excited and thanked us for opening our hearts to one more child. As I hung up the phone, Big Al giggled in his sleep. I'm pretty sure he knew what had just taken place. I closed my eyes and whispered a prayer thanking God for believing in us to care for one more of His children and thanked my grandfather for visiting me in my dream weeks earlier.

I have a large extended family, and every year we rent out the local 4-H campground and have a four-day family reunion. Hundreds of aunts, uncles, cousins, friends, moms, dads, grandmothers, and grandfathers gather together for four days of fun, food, fellowship, apple butter making, Saturday night family craft auction, playing the card game Spoons all night, Sunday-morning worship, and games. It is one of the highlights of my childhood and something I enjoy sharing with my own children.

That year, I was packing up our blankets and pillows and getting things ready to load in the car when my phone rang. The voice on the other end said, "Hello, this is Mrs. Jones. I am with the DHHR.

Are you the foster parents of Little Miss and Wild Man?" (She of course used their birth names.) I answered yes and asked what was going on. I knew something was wrong because no one used their birth names anymore. She assured me nothing was wrong and that in fact she was calling to let me know that their mom had given birth to a baby boy about three weeks earlier. He had gone home from the hospital with his father, but the situation had not worked out, and the state now had him in their care. She then said, "Seeing that you have his siblings and they are not adopted yet, we will be bringing him out to you this afternoon."

All I could get out of my mouth was, "We just took in a newborn. I don't think we can take him in without a waiver." My mind raced with questions as she explained what was taking place. Was this the reason the adoption had been moved and pushed back so many times? Was this really happening? What in the world was my husband going to say? Could we really handle two newborns, a three-year-old, a four-year-old, and our teens? My mind was spinning. I told her we were leaving for the weekend to go to our family reunion, that if she wanted us to have him that weekend, she would have to be at my house before four. She agreed, and in just a few hours, she carried in a very tiny little guy with big, wide eyes.

She carried his car seat over and sat it in the floor. He was sound asleep. Wild Man and Little Miss both quickly made their way over to see what the lady had brought in. Little Miss took one look at him and said, "Aw, it's baby Elmo." I laughed.

The worker then told me what his name was, and I looked back over at Little Miss and said, "Baby Elmo it is then." The worker went over what history she had on him and told me that I would need to get him in to see a doctor soon for his checkup. She then handed me paperwork saying we had permission to take him to the reunion. She said she knew we were in a hurry and that she would not keep us. She thanked us and headed out the door, saying if we needed anything to give her a call. She was in and out of my house in fifteen minutes.

My husband arrived and smiled as he saw me standing on the front porch with not one but two newborn babies. He walked up the sidewalk and kissed my cheek. "I see you've been busy today," he said with a chuckle. He smiled down at the newest addition to our home and said, "Pleased to meet you, little guy," and then started loading the car with our things for the reunion.

When we arrived at the reunion, my mom and cousin were anxiously waiting at our cabin to hold Big Al. When I stepped out of the car with not one but two babies, I was met with both smiles and laughter. They quickly came and took the little ones in the cabin as we unloaded our things. We had gone from a family of six to a family of eight in less than a month. Big Al and Elmo were quickly dubbed the twins by many because they are only eight days apart in age. Growing up, I had always wanted twins. I guess God found a way to make that dream possible. I have often wondered if God was laughing at my husband and me as we had that *we are finished with foster care* talk on the way to the store that one Saturday morning. We did not know His plans for us, but I am thankful He knew what He had in store for us. He is so good to us.

Our First Forever Family Day

> Every good gift and every perfect gift is from above,
> coming down from the Father of lights, with whom
> can be no variation, nor turning shadow.
> —James 1:17 (World English Bible)

Life with our two new little guys was going well—better than well, it was going great. I worried that adding two more to our daily lives might be overwhelming, but we were blessed to have an amazing support system. As we drew closer to the adoption date for Wild Man and Little Miss, we finalized plans for the celebration party. We decided to keep the party simple, immediate family and a few close friends. Then the day finally arrived. September 20, 2013, we officially became a forever family.

The morning started like any other morning, with the exception my husband did not go into work. I was woken up by the sounds of Wild Man running into my room and the light whimpers of baby Elmo trying his best not to wake with the morning light. Little Miss and Big Al were still fast asleep. I carried Wild Man downstairs and turned on the TV. I could not help the smile that was on my face. *Today he will finally have our last name*, I thought to myself. I went to the kitchen and prepared his morning cup of milk and made Elmo his morning bottle. As I went to get Elmo from his crib, Wild Man looked up at me and smiled. I think he knew that this day was going to be something special. I went and picked up Elmo and brought him downstairs, and we started off our morning.

Today was the day we had waited for. Today was the day that had been postponed and moved and at times we felt we would never reach. Today was adoption day. I looked at our little Wild Man and thought back to the day he came to us. He was so small and weak, and many thought he would not make it, but here he was sitting in our living room watching his favorite cartoon, drinking milk, and laughing his deep, old man laugh. For 818 days, I had held him and told him he would be all right. I had sat in hospital rooms waiting to hear if he had pulled through surgery after surgery. I had prayed for him daily. I had loved him and cared for him as if he were my own. I had fought for him when others had given up, I had fought for us to become his forever family, and today even though he had been my son from the moment I first held him, today it would be official. After 818 days of waiting, of not knowing, of fearing the unseen, and praying for the Lord's Will to be done, the wait was finally over. Eight hundred and eighteen days is too long for a child to wait for a family. I am so thankful he was with us the whole time.

Little Miss had been with us 719 days. Though the days were fewer, they were still too many. She had grown so much in her two years with us. She was no longer the shy little girl who did not talk or feed herself. Now she was a spunky and sometimes bossy little three-and-a-half-year-old that could talk a stranger's leg off, and the only food she would not eat was carrots. She was a completely different kid. I could not believe I was going to be her forever mom.

Finally, the rest of our beautiful chaos made their way down the stairs, and we all managed to get ready and made our way to the courthouse. As we unloaded the car, we were met by both my parents and my husband's parents. Once we arrived, we went through security and were told to head up to the courtroom. When we made it to the courtroom, we were greeted by a bailiff who told us the judge was still in with another case. He asked us to have a seat in the hallway and wait. And we did, for an hour and a half with a three-and-a-half-year-old, a two-and-a-half-year-old, two newborns, two teens, and a host of family members. Thank goodness, we brought snacks and a few little toys to keep them busy.

By the time we made our way into the courtroom Wild Man and Little Miss were restless. The judge made her way up to her bench, and we were sworn in. She apologized for taking so long with the other case before she started with ours. She said the day was a joyful day and she knew the children were tired of waiting, so she allowed them to roam freely in the courtroom. After we were sworn in, our lawyer asked which one of us wanted to speak. My very quiet husband nodded in my direction, and I agreed to do the talking. The questions were simple to answer: Do you love these children? Do you understand that this is a lifetime commitment? Do you understand that they will now be your responsibility? Do you promise to love and care for them as your own? Yes, yes, yes, and yes. Then I was asked to talk about our life and how Wild Man and Little Miss had made it different, how they had made it better. I did not plan on being so emotional, but as I told our story, tears ran down my face. As I watched them run around and spin in the floor, I giggled, as did everyone in the courtroom. Then the judge read over the petition, and with her gavel, she declared that on that day, September 20, 2013, Wild Man and Little Miss would be from now on known as JR and Elissa. I cried even harder.

We were asked if we wanted to take pictures to remember the day, and we of course said yes. The judge came down front and lined up with us and our family as friends and other family members took turns snapping photos of our now family of six. I then asked to have Big Al and Elmo brought up front, so we could get photos with them as well. The judge asked who the babies belonged to, and I laughed and told her us. I explained that we were still active foster parents and gave her their names. By the look on her face, I knew she recognized the names. As I explained their situations, she took in everything about the boys. She had been the judge throughout the entire process with Wild

Man and Little Miss, and she was now the judge over Elmo's case. She smiled and said she was glad we had agreed to keep the siblings together.

And just like that, we were a forever family. What had taken over two and a half years was finally finished, and they were now ours.

Life with Four under Four

> Let them be little, Cause they're only that way for a while. Give them hope, give them praise, give them love every day. Let 'em cry, let 'em giggle, let 'em sleep in the middle, Oh, but let them be little.
> —Billy Dean

Life with our four little ones kept us on our toes after the adoption. We were still getting accustomed to having the baby boys around and trying to manage our time wisely. Normal routine things such as going to church or going to the store seemed overwhelming at times, but we were making it.

JR, Wild Man, was now going to preschool Monday through Thursdays, and on Fridays he spent the morning with his OT, speech, and music therapists. His preschool teachers were absolutely wonderful with him. Both ladies were so sweet and caring and always made sure I received daily updates on his progress. They never looked at him as a child with special needs. They saw what I saw, a sweet lovable little guy destined to do great and mighty things. When he was with them, I did not worry; I knew they would take care of him and that he was safe with them. I imagine that's something every parent wants to feel while their child is at school.

Elissa, Little Miss, was now in kindergarten. She had loved her preschool teachers and was excited to be moving on up to the big school building. Her new teacher happened to be our oldest daughter and son's teacher when they attended the school years prior. Mrs. Jordan had decided that 2015 would be her last year teaching and planned on retiring at the end of the school year. I had to laugh when I thought back to the first time we had met. It was her first year at the school. Sierra was part of her first class, so it seemed fitting that our youngest daughter be part of her last class. I could not get over how much things had changed in the fifteen years since we first stepped foot in the school. While the building itself still looked the same, so many fresh faces walked the halls. Many of the teachers I had known had retired or transferred schools. A few were still there and smiled as I made my way down the hallway with our little girl. Some asked if she was my granddaughter, to which I laughed and said, "No, she's mine." I was pleased to find out one of Sierra's favorite teachers was now the school counselor, and the principal was still the same. I was blessed to be able to enroll them in the same school our older two had attended. It made it easier for them to know Mommy was friends with many of the teachers there. As the days turned into weeks and the weeks turned into months, the kids were both finding themselves and learning many new and exciting things.

As for the boys, Big Al and Elmo, they were both doing well. We spent the days between Birth to Three appointments and visits with their parents. The center where the supervised visits took place was kind enough to set up both boys' visits at the same time. That way I was not making several trips into town each week. The visits lasted two hours, so while they were visiting their parents, I had time to run and do errands if needed. Some days, I would take a book to read while I waited, or I would catch up on their life books. Some days, the visits seemed to last forever, while others passed by quickly.

The thing about supervised visits is that for them to work, both the child and the parent(s) must attend. Big Al had three visits before his birth mom started calling the visit off or showing up and leaving early. He had seen her a total of ten times before the visits come to a sudden stop. His mother had wanted to place him up for adoption from the beginning. She did not want to go through visitations or through the foster care process. For his safety, the visits were terminated.

As for Elmo, he had visits for six months with his mother and then a little over a year of visits with his father. His father was given extra time with him to determine if he was a suitable parent. His mother had already been terminated twice, so there was no chance of her getting him back, but the father had no prior terminations. So, for over a year, I loaded everyone up in the van and dropped off Elissa and JR to school and headed into town for his visit. When we arrived at the center, I kissed Elmo and handed him off to the worker and hoped for the best.

Big Al's case was simple in that his mother agreed to termination. That only left the father. A DNA test was performed on a couple of potential fathers, but in the end, neither turned out to be his father. As sad as it may sound, an ad in both the local and state newspapers was placed in search of "unknown father." The ad ran its required time, and when no potential father stepped forward, termination of unknown father occurred. He was free to move on to adoption in April 2014. Elmo's case was more challenging. His father deep down wanted his son, his only son, but he could not stay away from the mother. The court made it clear that for him to gain custody, he would have to stay away from her. After many failed attempts to stay away from her and a list of other unresolved requirements—maintain a job, provide adequate housing, and provide dependable childcare while he was at work—the court ordered his rights to be terminated.

My husband and I were traveling to see our first ever Green Bay Packer game at Lambeau Field when my phone rang. It was Elmo's caseworker. She was calling to let us know there had been an emergency hearing in the case earlier that morning. At that hearing, the judge had decided that Elmo's father had not completed the necessary steps to get his son back, therefore demonstrating he was not a suitable placement for the him. She was calling to ask us the all-important question, Would we be willing to keep Elmo with his half siblings? We agreed. We would officially become a family of eight. Elmo would grow up with his half sister and his half brother while gaining two new brothers, Big Al and Devin, and a big sister, Sierra. Talk about an exciting weekend. I told my husband we would have to enjoy our little mini getaway because it could be our last one for a while. We did enjoy our weekend. It was great to see the Packers play and win at Lambeau Field. It had been a lifelong dream of mine, and thanks to our new friends Jon and Nadine, it had finally come true. Before we headed home, I picked up new Packer clothing for all the kids. What better way to celebrate the big win and our win on becoming a family of eight than with new Packer clothing?

After we returned home from our trip, the process was started to move the boys from the foster care side to the adoption side. We filled out their child summaries and picked out their forever names, just as we had done with JR and Elissa. Our lives were moving at a fast pace, and we were loving it. We knew with the adoption of the boys; our family would be complete. I was ready to officially be a mom of six children. What a tremendous blessing. Each one had his or her own set of obstacles to overcome, but we were ready. We looked forward to helping the new little ones grow and could not wait to see them conquer daily challenges. God had not promised us life would be easy, but He did promise He would be forever faithful by our sides.

Sierra was now attending college, so she was no longer around to help with the day-to-day routine at home. Even with her not physically there, she still made time to call and check in daily and talk with her siblings and ask about their day. Devin was in high school, so his time was spent between taekwondo, marching band, concert band, jazz band, and homework. Our saxophone-playing son was very busy. He did, however, always make time for his little siblings. They loved to hear him practice his sax at home, and they loved it when he became their personal jungle gym. He had stepped up to help even more now that his sister was away. I am still amazed at how well our big kids adjusted to having the little ones around. I don't know many teens who would give up their evenings to play matchbox cars, or to watch cartoons, or to build forts in the middle of our living room so their brothers and sister could go "camping," but ours did. They were the perfect big sister and big brother. The little ones were, and still are, blessed to have such loving older siblings. They both, however, have informed me that I will not be a grandmother anytime soon because they have changed their fair share of dirty butts and they understand that babies are serious work. The ultimate birth control for teens in my book.

Forever Family Day, Take Two

> He took a little child, and set him in the middle of them.
> Taking him in his arms, he said to them, "Whoever receives
> one such little child in my name, receives me, and whoever
> receives me, doesn't receive me but him who sent me."
> —Mark 9:36–37 (World English Bible)

If adoption has taught us anything, it's been a huge lesson on how to be patient. There is a process that must be followed, court dates must take place, forms must be filed and refiled, visitations must happen if the child is in foster care, all family members must be ruled out as possible forever homes, and birth parents are given chance after chance to improve their situation (reunification with the birth parents is always the goal). That is hard for many people, including foster parents, to understand. We go to court time after time and see little to no improvement, and we, as foster parents, get aggravated and angry that the judge gives the parents "one more improvement period." We pray that the birth parents will straighten up and get their lives back in order, even if it means losing the child we have come to love. Deep down, if we are honest with ourselves, we also pray that the child does not have to return to the uncertain mess they came from. We pray they can stay with us or that they can be adopted by another foster-to-adopt family. Or at least that's how I have felt on more than one occasion. There are days that you wonder if reunification will ever happen, and then when you realize it will not, you start to wonder if the adoption will ever happen. The process is long and draining at times. There are many sleepless nights, and there are days of nothing but worry and sadness, but then sometimes there come days of extraordinary joy and celebration.

Six hundred and seventy days and 692 days. Those are the number of days that Elmo and Big Al were in foster care. The number of days we held them, that we prayed over them, that we worried, that we cried for them, that we cared for them, that we fed them, bathed them, played with them, took them to the doctors' appointments and specialist appointments, took them to church and family vacations; those are the number of days we had to fall in love with them before they became forever ours. Almost two years they were in the system. They were considered lucky in that they were never moved from home to home. They were considered lucky in that they were getting adopted. Lucky, such an odd word to use when talking about foster care. The truth is they could have had it much worse. Many children in foster care do. They are bounced from foster home to foster home and spend years in the system only to age out with no family to call their own. The average length of time a child spends in foster care is over two years, with 6 percent having stays longer than five years, according to research by the Children's Rights Group.

Here are some other facts about foster care according to the Children's Rights Group, Administration for Children and Families, and FosterClub:

- There is an average of over 428,000 children in foster care on any given day in the United States (CRG).
- The average age of a child in foster care is nine (CRG).
- Over 20,000 children aged out (turned eighteen) in 2015 with no one to call family, leaving them to live on the streets or in shelters (CRG).

- The number of children in foster care increased by 13 percent in 2015 (ACF).
- One in 184 children in the United States is in foster care (ACF).
- Of those in care, 52 percent are males and 48 percent are females (ACF).
- The number of children who enter foster care every year is 264,746 (that's one child every two minutes in the United States) (FC).
- Around 108,000 are waiting to be adopted (FC).

So, I guess luck would be the word many would use. Those facts and figures are scary. I never knew so many children here in the United States were in need until I became a foster parent. I lived in an imaginary world where I assumed all children had a loving mom or dad to tuck them in at night. I never dreamt that there were so many children just waiting to have a place to call home or that so many would age out with nobody to love them or a place to stay. It was all part of God's plan to open our eyes to the need for good, loving foster parents. Our boys were placed with us as soon as the state became involved, and we were the ones blessed to have them in our home from the moment they went into the system. We were blessed that God called us to be their foster parents and then to be their forever parents. And on a warm day in the middle of June, we became a forever family of eight.

June 17, 2015, we arrived at the courthouse a little early. We were greeted by our family and friends. We had Birth to Three workers, who were now considered some of our closest friends, there. We had old caseworkers and old staff workers there. The courtroom was full of people. They were there to celebrate with us, to welcome in our newest additions. That's what it's all about. Celebrating the life of the child, the blessing that God had given us. To celebrate the love and joy these two precious boys brought to our lives. Surrounded by a room full of love, we went up front and stated our case as to why we wanted to adopt the boys. Our lawyers asked the questions as they had in our first adoption: Do you love this child? Do you understand this is a lifelong commitment? Do you promise to care for and provide for this child as your own? And again, I promised myself I would not cry. I lied again. As I talked about the two little boys, my boys, the tears flowed down my cheeks. When I was younger, I had dreamt of having twins, and that dream had fallen short until now. God had made a way, as only He could, to give me my twins.

True, they were not actual twins, but being only eight days apart, they were close enough. They talked in their own language, they sat up days apart from each other, they crawled hours apart from each other, and they even started walking days apart. In every sense of the word, they were twins, and they were almost ours forever. The thought that God was allowing us to adopt again was overwhelming. As the judge smiled down and ordered from that day forward the boys would be known as Alex and Eli, I cried even harder. We were not worthy of God's blessings, but we were so thankful He had given us favor in our journey as foster parents. We took pictures with our new sons and our family. We took pictures with the judge, with our extended family, and with all our friends who showed up to celebrate with us. Life was not good but great. The judge joked with us and asked if we were finished growing our family with these two precious boys. With smiles on our faces, we said, "Yes, our family is complete."

I can't help but think God was looking down at us and laughing, once again saying, "Oh, my child. We are not finished just yet."

The Job Transfer

> Yahweh our God spoke to us in Horeb, saying, "You have lived long enough at this mountain."
> —Deuteronomy 1:6 (World English Bible)

With the boys' adoptions finalized, we felt our lives were complete and life was good—nothing but blue skies in our future. However, my husband's job had other plans. Work had been anything but easy over the last few months. He was working a lot of overtime doing runs/deliveries that no one else wanted to do. And even though he had been with the company awhile, he was stuck in the same position with little hope of moving up. He was getting frustrated, and truth be told, so was I. He was working so hard for the company and for us. I hated seeing him so miserable. He went out before the kids were up and came home many nights after they were fast asleep. It was getting old, and he knew he needed a change. We talked about him finding another job, we talked about him starting his own business, and we talked about everything in between. We prayed for God to open doors, and we prayed for understanding. Then one day we received an answer to our prayers. One of the branch bosses was in town and asked my husband how things were going. My husband, who is usually a man of few words, told him exactly how it was going and how aggravated he was getting with his job. The branch boss was surprised that my husband was still only a truck driver and asked if he had ever thought about transferring to a different location.

When my husband made it home that night, we had another long talk. Transferring to a different location meant moving away from our family and friends. To me, it meant leaving the only area I had ever called home. In my forty years, I had moved a few times, but I remained within twenty-mile ratios from where I had grown up and where my parents still to this day live. We talked and prayed about the possibilities all night and decided if it was what was best for our family, that's what we would do.

It's funny how fast things move after you hand them over to God. We had spent over a year worrying and trying to figure things out about his job, and nothing changed. And as soon as we fully turned our worries over to God, things began to move. Within a few weeks, my husband was informed about a position opening in Florida. I think he knew what I was going to say before he even asked me about it, but he asked anyway. I was coming to terms with the fact that we may have to move away, but I was not ready to move *that* far away. If he took that position, we would be more than fifteen hours away from our parents, from our friends, and from our oldest daughter who was in college in West Virginia. The look on my face told him what he already knew. Florida was a no. He then started watching job postings on the company's webpage. Over the next few weeks, there were openings in South Carolina, North Carolina, and, if I remember correctly, New Jersey. While I do love the Carolinas, the sun, the ocean, the sights, I could not help but feel those places were not right for our family. We did discuss each opportunity and laid out the pros and cons, but ultimately, he did not pursue any of those positions. God had other plans.

While at work one day, Todd received a call from the boss he had spoken with a few months prior. He had a position, a driver position, opening in Tennessee. He knew my husband did not want to stay a driver forever; however, this was an opportunity to get him in at a new branch, and he would be able to move up the company ladder.

My husband called and told me what his boss had offered, and we agreed to talk about it later that evening after he made it home. That afternoon, I tried to come up with a list of cons (forgive me, Lord) as to why Tennessee would not work for us either. I tried the "It's too far away" and the "But the kids will miss the snow" excuses we had used on a few of the other jobs, but with Tennessee, those excuses would not work. We vacationed in Gatlinburg several times a year, and we have season tickets to the racetrack in Bristol. We could make the trip to Tennessee in our sleep. What to do? What to do? When he arrived home that night and after we had tucked all the little ones in bed, we had another talk. This one would change our lives. We agreed he should try the position in Tennessee out and see what happened. He discussed it with his boss the next day, and they agreed he could go down and work a few weeks and see what he thought before making any major decisions. We prepared ourselves and the kids as best we could. We stocked up on groceries, we went over doctor appointments and meetings, and we made sure the kids understood that Daddy was going to be gone for a little while for work. It took a few weeks to get everything in order, but on a Sunday afternoon in early September, he made his way down to a hotel in Tennessee, so he could start work bright and early Monday morning. Those two weeks seemed to drag by, but we survived. My husband loved the more relaxed work environment. It was clear to me when I spoke with him in the evenings that he was happier there. How could I say no? The decision was made, he would take the job. We would work something out. We agreed I would stay in West Virginia until school was out with the kids, and he would come home on the weekends. Not ideal, I know, but our oldest son was a senior. I wanted him to graduate with his friends and classmates. I had my son, my parents, and in-laws to help me with the routine things with the kids during the week while he was gone if need be. It would be hard on all of us, but it was nine months. We could do it.

And Then Came Baby

> A new baby is like the beginning of all things
> wonder, hope, a dream of possibilities.
> —Eda J. LeShan

I believe God talks to us in our dreams. I believe He tells us things while we sleep that He knows we would dismiss if we were awake. And I believe He gives us dreams to give us a glimpse of what He has in store for us.

For Sierra's birthday, I bought us tickets to a women's conference. We loved this particular conference, and I enjoyed quality time with my oldest. The worship music was always outstanding, and the messages brought by the speakers seemed to always be just what we needed to hear. When I told her we were going, she was excited. With all the little ones and her away at college now, we didn't get much one-on-one mom/daughter time. I was looking forward to our girls' weekend. A few days later, I had a dream. In the dream, there was a little girl with brown hair in pigtails. I could not make out her face well, but oh, I remember that smile. What a smile she had—and that laugh, such a precious sound. Over the next few days and weeks, this little girl's image continued to return to me. I knew it was not of either one of my daughters. Sierra was now grown, and Elissa had very blonde hair. I told Sierra about the dream on the way to the conference, and she was just as puzzled as I was.

We made it to the conference, and there was a table set up to sponsor children overseas who were in danger or in need. We walked by the table a few times, and then after a very moving message from one of the speakers, we went back to take another look. There my daughter found a little girl she felt called to help. She provided the necessary information to sponsor her, and we turned to walk away. That's when I saw the folder with a little girl's picture on it. She was about the same age as Elissa. She had dark hair, and it was in pigtails. I looked at Sierra and asked her if she thought the little girl could be the girl from my dream. She said anything was possible. So I became her sponsor. But the imagines of the little girl in my dreams did not stop; in fact, they intensified.

It was mid-September, and my husband was in for the weekend and wanted to go look at campers. His new job was paying for a hotel room until he could find something more permanent, but he did not want them to have to do that for long. With his new schedule and mine back home, there had not been time to look at apartments or houses in the area. So, he decided that a new camper was needed. He could use the camper to stay in until we could find a house, and after we moved, we could use it to stay in when we came back to visit family. Sounded logical to me. We loaded the kids up and headed out in search of the perfect camper for our family. We were about an hour and a half into our trip when my phone rang. I looked but did not recognize the number. I showed it to my husband, and he shook his head; he didn't recognize it either. Two of our children were with his parents. They had taken them to a farm where they could pet goats and ride horses. I looked at my husband and said, "Could it be your parents? Maybe something happened, and they don't have their phones."

He replied, "Maybe," so I answered it.

On the other end, a lady's voice said, "Hello. My name is Ms. Maxwell. I'm with the department. Do you have a second?" My heart sank. The look on my face must have said it all. I looked at my husband, and he instantly knew who was on the other end of that phone call. He started shaking his head no, and I sat there and took in what she was trying to say, all while trying to find a subtle way to tell her, "No, we are full and in the process of moving. We can't take in another child."

Then she said, "She had another baby, a baby girl. The mom says she is the full sibling to your youngest son. She is signing herself out of the hospital. We have already taken custody of baby girl. I was hoping to place her with you. Would you be willing to take the baby?" I told her to give me a minute, that I would need to talk it over with my husband. I would call her back in a few minutes.

I got off the phone, and both our oldest son and husband were now shaking their heads no. I looked over, and his eyes met mine, and I said, "She had another baby. It's a girl." He looked at me and let out a sigh, and his head stopped shaking no.

After a few moments, he said, "Okay. How can we say no? But we still need to go look at campers. See if we can pick her up later this evening." I called the worker back and told her we would take her in. I explained that we were looking at campers at the time and it would be later that evening before we could make it down to the hospital. She said that would be fine; it would take a while to get all the paperwork in order. She asked me to call when we were headed that way, so she could meet us at the hospital. She then asked me to come up with a name; as far as anyone knew, the mom had not given baby girl a name.

We drove the rest of the way to the camper lot. We got out and walked around, but our minds were on baby girl. We did look at a few campers but quickly made our way back to the car and headed home. I called my parents and asked if they could come down and watch the little ones while we went to the hospital. My mother laughed and said we were nuts but agreed to come down and watch the kids for us. When we arrived at our house, she and my dad were waiting in the driveway. We unloaded the little ones and quickly changed diapers and made sure they were fed. Then we headed to the hospital.

When we arrived, we were buzzed in and escorted to her room. The nurse had found a piece of paper that had the baby's name on it. Her mom had decided to name her before she left the hospital. They asked us what name we had picked out, and we told them Sadie Mae.

She was to be named in honor of two of our grandmothers. Sadie means princess in Hebrew, and she was to be our new little princess. The nurse then told us they would call her Sadie from then on. She told us baby girl was doing well considering her circumstances. She was born early and had some drugs in her system, so she would have to stay in the hospital for a few more days, which meant she would not be going home with us that evening. As the nurse opened the door, she asked us, "Are you ready to meet your daughter?" They wheeled her little bed over for us to see, and there wrapped in a white blanket was the sweetest little brown-haired girl I had even seen. I felt God in that moment, and I knew she was the one He had given me the vision of. I picked her up, all four pounds and nine ounces of her, and held her in my arms. My husband walked over and smiled down and said, "She sure is prettier than any camper we looked at today." He kissed my forehead and smiled. We were on our way to becoming a family of nine.

We spent as much time as possible at the hospital over the next few days. Sadie, or peanut as she was nicknamed, was getting stronger much faster than the doctors and nurses had originally thought. And after only a week in NICU, she was up to five pounds and was cleared to come home. We drove to the hospital and were greeted by the nursing staff that had taken care of her. They knew she was going home and had pooled their money together to buy her a few things. In her gift bag, she had a few outfits, some diapers, and a pink elephant blanket. They took turns coming by her room as we were organizing the final paperwork for her discharge. The nursing staff wished us luck, told her goodbye, and posed for a group picture. We were given a new car seat, courtesy of the hospital, and then she was discharged. Heading home, I could not stop looking back at her. After we got her home and introduced her to her brothers and sister, I sent her caseworker a text letting her know we had her home and that I had already spoken with our pediatrician's office. They were happy to take her on as a new patient. I asked when visitations would start with her parents and when the first court hearing would be. She told me she would be out in a few days to see her, and by then she should have all the information I needed. She was true to her word.

Peanut's case was not like her sister or brother's cases. Since the mom and dad had parental rights terminated less than a year prior and their circumstances had not improved, there were no weekly visitations ordered. The judge ordered one visit when she was about three months old, allowing her parents to say their goodbyes. The first hearing was scheduled, and I found myself in the familiar hallway waiting. As I sat on that wooden bench outside the courtroom doors, the elevator door opened, and baby girl's parents stepped off. Her mom looked over and saw me. She forced a half smile. As she walked toward me, she said, "I was hoping I would see you here." Eli's biological dad made his way over as well and ask me if he could ask how his son was doing. I told him that he was doing fine and shared a few stories. He smiled. As fate would have it, the court case in front of theirs was running over, so we all sat on the bench and made small talk. They asked if I had any new pictures of the kids that I could show them, so I pulled out my phone. The three of us sat and looked at pictures of both baby girl and Eli. After a few minutes, he got up and walked over to talk with his lawyer. She looked at me and said, "They sure are growing up, aren't they?" And then she sighed. "Could you show me a picture of my other two?" I froze for a moment. She had not seen either of them in over two and a half years. The last time she had seen JR, he was hooked up to a machine and a feeding tube. I honestly was not sure I was completely comfortable with her seeing pictures of them now. But then I looked in her eyes and thought to myself, *It's just a photo.* She just wanted to catch a glimpse of them. In that moment, my heart hurt for her. I could not imagine not having my kids with me. I could feel the pain she was feeling. Yes, I know she brought it all on herself and that the situation could have played out much differently for her if she had chosen a different path, but in that moment, all I saw was a mom wanting to see how much her kids had grown. So, I pulled my phone back out and scrolled through a few photos, allowing her to see how happy all four of her kids were. She smiled. The courtroom doors opened, and it was time for them to go in.

Sadie's case moved much faster than the previous two adoptions. Maybe it's because God knew we were moving or maybe we were just fortunate this time; either way, it moved quickly. We had only one MDT (multidisciplinary team) meeting and one more court hearing. At the MDT, I sat with my notepad filled with all the information the lawyers and court liaison normally asked for: who is the child staying with, how is the child doing in this environment, are there visitations with the birth parents, and if so, how are they going, and some basic information such as how much does the child weigh, is the child physically okay, and is there any reason to move the child from this home. As I sat in the small room listening to all the voices talk around me, I realized what the plan was for this precious baby girl long before it was announced. Her birth parents made their case as to why they should get her back, but it did no good. Their story had not changed since they lost their son, my now two-year-old. It was the same excuses and the same lies. In fact, part of the reason the father had lost custody of his son was due to the fact he could not stay away from the mother. The team agreed that in light of there being a new child involved that the two were still together and agreed to move forward with the termination of parental rights. There were several other circumstances that were involved, but those are not mine to discuss. I did not have to say a word. The whole situation played out in front of me, and all I could think was, *This is really happening. She is really going to stay with us.* At the end of the meeting, I was given our next court date.

Finding a Place to Call Home

A house is made with walls and beams; a
home is built with love and dreams.
—Ralph Waldo Emerson

My husband was settled into his new job, and we agreed it was time to start looking for a house to call home. My parents came over one weekend in December to watch the kids so that I could go on our first house hunt in Tennessee. I had contacted a real estate agent and given her a list of properties we would like to see, and she in turn pulled a few she thought would fit what we were looking for. I made it to my husband's hotel room around five in the morning. We went to breakfast, and I caught him up on all the latest things the kids were into, and we set out to meet the Realtor. She was about our age and sweet as could be. She told us her game plan for the next two days and which houses we were going to see. We talked about clogging (an Appalachian dance style), doughnuts, and Jesus. She was definitely my type of Realtor. We looked at the first few houses, and nothing really stood out. I was not expecting to find "the one" on our first try, but I was disappointed in what we had seen. Then she brought us to one that we had both liked on a Realtor app. We pulled up, and there in the garage was a man working on a handmade bed for his son's birthday. She asked if it was okay for us to have a look around, and he said it was fine. He apologized for being there; he was the homeowner's son-in-law, and he was not aware of the showing that day. We talked to him and his dad for a few minutes, and he filled us in on what he knew about the house before we made our way inside. It was even better than the pictures on the website. I was in love. My husband even liked it. There were enough bedrooms for everyone, there was a playroom for the massive number of toys that come with having five smaller children, there was a decent-size yard, and there were three bathrooms (thank you, Jesus). We thanked the son-in-law for answering questions, and we headed off to the next house.

Later that evening when we were back at the hotel, we started going through the listings and making a pros and cons list for each. Some of the houses we were able to throw out immediately, some we liked the location, some we liked the size, but none compared to the one the son-in-law talked up. The only problem with that one was price. We talked and prayed about it that evening and asked our Realtor if we could see it again before I headed back home. She agreed, and we went back over early the next morning. As we walked through the home, I could picture the kids running around in the toy room. I picked out what rooms I figured the children would claim as their own, and for the first time since we thought about moving, I was excited. We drove back to the hotel, and I kissed my husband goodbye. I loaded up in the car and headed home. *There was no way we found our house on the first visit*, I thought to myself. But I could not shake the idea of that one being ours. When I got home and settled in, I called my husband, and he agreed we needed to at least submit an offer and see what happened. Our comfort budget and the price of the house differed by a rather sizable amount. We prayed about it and settled on an offer price. It was much lower than the list price, but it was the best we could do. We crossed our fingers and hoped for the best.

When God has His hands in the plan, things happen. And that's exactly what happened for us. We call it our Christmas miracle. The kids and I were watching TV, in middle of one of the largest snowstorms I can recall, and my phone rang. It was our Realtor.

Beautiful Chaos

She asked, "Are you sitting down?" I figured our offer had insulted the owners and told her yes and asked what was going on. She said, "Congratulations, you just bought a house! They accepted your offer." I could not believe it. She stated that the owners agreed to our price without a counteroffer. Their son-in-law had told them about us and our large family. The house had been on the market for a few months, and the owners were selling because they were now caring for the husband's mother. They didn't have time to keep up with an empty house. They told her to tell us Merry Christmas and to enjoy the house as much as they had. The wife's father had built the house back some twenty years ago for her family. She hated to sell it but knew they needed to. She wanted it to go to a family that could really use the space and one that would make many happy memories there, just as her family had done over the years. When they received our offer, she was glad the house would be full of little ones again. The son-in-law had even told them about my husband living out of the hotel for work, and they agreed to let him move in before closing. Can you say God is good!

I quickly called my husband and told him the news. A few weeks later, he was at our house picking up furniture we could survive without for a few months and taking it down to our new home. God had given us favor. No one can tell me that our move was not what God had planned for us. We found a house on our first outing, the sellers agreed to our offer, the schools in the area were exactly what we needed for all our children, and Sadie's adoption was moving at record speed. God was moving, and He was moving fast. As my husband started getting things ready down in Tennessee, I was working on wrapping things up back home. Our oldest son was in his senior year. We had final band concerts, college tours, and all things that made up senior year. Our preschooler and kindergartener were busy with activities as well, and we had regular meetings to discuss what type of classes or programs would be best for them at their new schools. Our two youngest boys were enjoying daycare a few days a week while I worked on packing, and of course there were all the things going on with baby girl. In March, we took a break from all the stress and spent the kids' spring break at the new house, so the kids could see their dad and so we could see what the area had to offer. Life was good.

Adoption Number Three

> Ohana means family. Family means nobody
> gets left behind or forgotten.
> —Disney's Lilo and Stitch

Soon we found ourselves back at the courthouse for another hearing for baby girl. I was sitting on the old wooden bench when the elevator doors opened, and her birth parents walked in. By this time, we were on friendly terms. They both half-smiled and walked over to talk with their lawyer. I sat and played a game on my phone. A few minutes later, she walked over and took the seat beside me and asked how things were going. I gave her an update on all the kids. Then out of nowhere, she thanked me. She said she was grateful that most of her kids were under one roof. We have four of her five. She told me that she was really trying to get her life in order. We talked for a few more minutes, and she asked if I would continue to pray for her and her situation. I of course said yes. She smiled and nodded her head. Then she asked me, "Will you promise to love my kids as if they were your kids?"

I replied, "I already do."

With that, she smiled again. Then, as if the two were taking turns talking to me, the dad came over. His eyes met mine, and in a teary plea, he asked, "If we agree not to fight this, will you keep the little girl with my boy?" I could see the pain in his face. I nodded my head and told him I would do everything in my power to keep them together. He thanked me, wiped a tear from his eye, and walked over to her. The hearing was short, less than fifteen minutes. When the doors opened, they both looked over at me and half-smiled one last time.

"I told the judge I knew my babies were in a loving home, and if I have another, I know he or she will be just as loved." Those were the last words I heard her say as the elevator door closed.

By that time, baby girl's lawyer was walking out. "They were terminated, and they agreed not to fight it. She will be all yours if you will have her."

It all felt like a dream. We would have to wait the allotted time for them to appeal, just in case they changed their minds, but it looked like she would be forever ours much sooner than any of her siblings. I sat in the hallway a few minutes while the lawyer and the caseworker talked with the judge's secretary about the next hearing date. They came back out and walked over to me. "This will be the next hearing. We will wait and see if they appeal. If not, we will move her over to the adoption side of things." I thanked them both and walked over to the elevator. When the doors opened, I sighed in relief; it was almost over. I called my husband and told him what had happened. We did some quick math, and we figured she would be officially ours by midsummer. That would be here soon—really soon.

The next couple of months flew by. My days were filled with our oldest son's senior activities, such as his last band concert, getting his tuxedo for prom, awards day, senior recognition day, and graduation practice. Elissa and JR both had things going on at the school as well, pre-k graduation, field day, and book fairs. Our year was quickly winding down. I continued attending our foster parent support group meetings and tried to help with the kids' activities at school, while at the house we were in full packing-up-to-move mode. My husband would come up every couple of weekends and pick up another load of furniture or clothing to take to our new place.

Before we knew it, we were in May. Early one morning, our

phone rang. It was our lawyer. "We have a date. June 27. Does that work for you all?" I told her yes, that worked just fine for us. We talked about a few other tiny details and hung up. I quickly called our caseworker. We were not planning a family vacation that year; instead, we decided to spend our "vacation" getting the new house in order. With the adoption date a little later than we had thought, we would need travel papers to take baby girl with us. She told me there would not be a problem getting them to me and said she would place them in the mail later that day. By mid-May, our son Devin was walking across the stage receiving his high school diploma. The last week of May, our son JR was receiving his certificate for completing pre-k. I cried like a baby at both ceremonies. Here we were, one finishing high school and one knocking on the door to start elementary school. It was nothing less than humorous. The sacrifice had been worth it to see them both graduate with their friends and classmates. The year had been so hard, both physically and emotionally, with my husband out of town working, but we had made it. And soon, very soon, we would all be under one roof again.

We spent our vacation getting the new house in order. The kids all picked out which room would be theirs and what colors the rooms would eventually be painted. We unpacked box after box of long-lost treasures we had nearly forgotten about and even managed to do a little sightseeing. Our vacation flew by. When it was time to go back home, the kids did not want to leave. They had enjoyed being with their dad every day, and so had I. It was nice having him around again for bath times and other dad duties. We sat them down and told them that in just a few short weeks, Sadie's adoption would be final, and then we could move. We loaded up and headed north to what would be our last few weeks as West Virginians.

June 27, 2016. Adoption day. We loaded up the van and headed to the courthouse. We were met once again by family, friends, and caseworkers who had all come to see our family grow by one. As we took pictures and shared stories in the hallway, I could feel God's presence in the moment. We were surrounded by people who loved us and who loved our kids, all of our kids. We were blessed to have our first home finder there as well as some of our old caseworkers. Everyone had come out to see us as our foster care journey in West Virginia ended with the adoption of this precious baby girl. They were there because we followed God's plan for us and agreed to open our home once again. After all, *what's one more?* We were blessed by the number of people who came out to share in this special day. When it was time, the judge called us into the courtroom, where again I stated why we loved this child and why we wanted her to be part of our forever family. The hearing was short and sweet. After a few questions and a few tear-filled replies, the judge declared that on that day, baby girl would be forever known as Sadie Mae. It was over. She was forever ours.

After the adoption, we went and ate dinner with my parents, then packed up the last of our boxes. A few hours after the adoption, we set out for our new home as a family of nine.

Our First Year in Our New Home

When we arrived at our new home, summer was in full swing. The idea of moving without my oldest children in tow made my heart ache, but they were young adults ready to start their own walks of life. I could not expect them to give up their dreams to move with us. Our oldest daughter knew I was having a tough time and wanted to make things a little easier for me. She surprised us by deciding to spend that summer with us to help us get settled into our new life in Tennessee. I was grateful. I had to have another surgery a few weeks before we moved. This one was to replace the batteries in my two SCSs. So, having her here to help with the kids was a godsend. I knew it would most likely be her last full summer with us before she set off to work in Washington, DC, so I was excited to have her join us. Our oldest son planned to live with my parents, so he could start college in the fall. He managed to make a few trips that summer to see us, which always made us and his little siblings happy. My life felt complete on those days I had all seven of the kids under one roof.

    Our first few months were spent getting to know the area. We figured out which back roads to take to bypass the traffic. We picked out a favorite grocery store and found the local Walmart. We explored the parks and local scenery. We located the kids' new schools and a few playgrounds. We even spent a few weekends at the local zoo and enjoyed the sunshine from the comforts of our backyard. We were getting into a routine, and life was coming together. The best part was getting to see my husband every evening again.

Todd had started attending a church he thought would be a good fit for our family. It was much like the one we attended before the move. The pastor was about our age, full of passion, and brought the Word to life in his messages. The church had a live band that played during worship, and it was nondenominational. They even had a coffee bar out in the foyer for those Sunday mornings we were running too late to make coffee at the house. At the sign-up station, there was a list of programs and projects the outreach services of the church participated in. The children's wing and staff welcomed our children with open arms. Elissa quickly made friends with the family pastor's daughter, while Alex and Eli were happy to be in the same class. Sadie loved all the attention she received in the nursery. I worried most about JR fitting in. Kids his own age tended to make fun of him or were easily annoyed with him due to his autism. This had been a problem at our old church. I knew being in the same class as Elissa, where he had to sit and read out of the Bible, would not work for him. So, we opted to place him in the class for older toddlers and preschool kids.

The last four years at our old church, Todd and I had spent the services apart. He had been talked into running the sound system, which he did not mind, but after four years of not getting to be with me in the pew, the toll had started to take effect. Worship was something we enjoyed together. I, on the other hand, was in the nursery and toddler room more than in the pew. While the room was set up so the worker could see and hear the service, if there were more than a few toddlers in class, the noise from them playing quickly became louder than the pastor over the speakers. We were on a rotation in the nursery room; however, I had three in the class. If JR got upset or nervous, I had to go and be with him. Nobody could handle his meltdowns. It was easier to just stay with him than for me to try to sneak out. He would get upset if I was not in there with him. And then there were our younger boys. Our family made up half of the class most days, so I guess others assumed it was my job to be in there. I was told on more than one occasion JR's meltdowns upset the other children and some of their parents, so if he was in there, I needed to be as well. To make things easier on everyone, I chose to stay. I wanted our children in church, and if that meant me sitting with them in the nursery, then so be it. But I missed sitting by my husband hand in hand worshipping our Lord. I needed that time with him.

So, when Todd introduced me to the new church, I was a bit apprehensive about JR being in a Sunday school class. The first few visits, Todd or I stayed with him. By the end of our first month, however, his teacher said she thought he would do okay without us. She took my cell phone number and said if she needed me, she would send a text or have the aide come get me. I was nervous but agreed to go with my husband to the sanctuary. I would love to say JR did great and I was not needed, but that would be a lie. When he realized we were not with him, he climbed the gate and took off down the hall. His teacher quickly caught up to him and took him back to class. He did have a meltdown, complete with screaming, kicking, and throwing himself against the floor. So, I was surprised I did not get a text saying, *Come get your child now!* Instead, my husband and I enjoyed the service, not knowing what our precious little guy was putting his new teacher through. When service was over, we headed over to the children's wing to pick up our little ones. When I went to JR's room, the teacher smiled and explained to me what had taken place. I found myself apologizing and asking if he was okay and if she was okay. With a warm smile, she took my hand and said, "It's fine. He is fine. This will be fine." She had not been scared off by the tornado of emotions that our son had been; in fact, she was determined, more than ever, to make him feel safe and loved while he was there. I thanked her for being so kind, and we walked to pick up the rest of our kids.

Autism can make the simplest of things unobtainable. The normal daily things like going to the store, or church, or out to eat, or even a family reunion can be too much for him to process. As we loaded up the Yukon, I looked over at my husband and told him I thought this could be our church. His teacher and aide did not have to keep him in the class; they could have easily come and gotten me when he was in middle of his meltdown. But they didn't. Instead, they showed him love and compassion. He *loves* going to church now. I am forever grateful to the staff. They love him, disability and all.

During our first year in Tennessee, we learned a lot about our children's disabilities and about how others react to them. Autism and RAD are part of our everyday lives. People tend to shy away from the subject of disability. Our children are so much more that the label they have been given. To understand us, I will share a little background on both before I continue our story.

JR was sick from the day he was placed with us. From the surgeries, to the chronic ear infections, his stomach issues, and everything in between, there was no doubt he was a very ill little boy. By the age of two, we noticed there was more going on than just his ever-changing illnesses. Yes, he had delays stemming from his neglected beginning, but there was more to it. I tried to dismiss it when he did not walk or talk as others his age did. I tried to play it off as if he were behind because of all the surgeries. But by the age of three, we had a diagnosis of autism. He spent his days lining up cars from front to back, all color coded with the smallest to the largest. He would sit and spin in circles for hours and repeated words like dada in threes. The early days, we were lost and had no idea how to help him.

He had a wonderful group of doctors and therapists who worked with him weekly to help him achieve what is now our normalcy. He met with his speech therapist, his OT, and his music therapist every Friday back in West Virginia. Before he started school, he had a team of amazing Birth to Three workers who provided OT, speech, and a list of other services. When he started preschool, he was blessed with amazing teachers who genuinely cared for him. I could not have asked for better teachers if I had handpicked them. So, moving to a city where I knew no one scared me. I had no idea which OT to take him to or what school setting would be best for him. I was lost and scared. He was now five, so he would not qualify for early intervention services, and without his team here to help me sort things out, I felt overwhelmed. Thankfully, Elissa's new school counselor came to my rescue.

We sat down for a face-to-face meeting, an IEP, to come up with a plan that would best suit his needs. The principal, teachers from a few different schools, a counselor, speech and OT therapists, my husband, and I sat around a table to discuss our little guy's future. I was impressed with the amount of information they had gathered about him; his preschool teachers had sent a very detailed account of his daily needs. The different teachers asked questions, and I answered and asked a few of my own. In the course of two hours, we had decided which school we felt best fit his needs. Even though the school that our daughter and younger boys would attend had a program that could work for JR, the idea of placing him in a regular kindergarten class and pulling him out throughout the day for extra help was not appealing to us. He did not do well with change, and making him go in and out of class all day would not work well for him or those trying to teach him. So, we decided on the school that hosted an autism classroom, and lucky for us, it was minutes from my husband's job. The teacher for that school invited us to come by so she could show us around and get more information on him.

I won't lie. I was a nervous wreck. I was not crazy about having our kids in two different schools. How would we make it to family fun nights at two schools? What if the school pickup times overlapped? What about bus pickups? Would they even be able to ride the bus? A list of questions and concerns flooded my mind. That is until I walked in the classroom.

It was exactly what I had searched for back home but had been unable to find. The first thing I noticed was the blue filters. The filters softened bright fluorescent lights, which would help tremendously with his sensitivity to light. There was a calmness about the room that made even me feel welcomed. It had an OT room off to the right of the classroom where the kids, if needed, could go for OT and to just release tension. There were large foam building blocks, a trapeze swing, a small rock wall, and countless other toys used for OT and gross motor skills training. It also had what she called a calming room. In there, the lights were turned down, and the kids had a choice of a disco ball light or a lamp that projected fish on the ceiling. My dad had bought the same fish light for JR's bedroom at the house. There were books, a crawl-through tunnel, quiet toys, and music. I could see JR relaxing in there if he were to have a meltdown in class. This was the type of room I dreamed of having in our own home. The class even had their own kitchen area and their own bathroom. I would not have to worry about him running off if he did decide to use the bathroom, and I could send in popcorn for him to eat for lunch. I wish every school had this type of setup for special-needs kids. I was in awe. And for once, I was excited for him to start school. His soon-to-be teacher asked us a few questions about his diet and if he was potty-trained. And for the first time, we were not met with the "What do you mean he's five and still in pull-ups?" question or the "He still eats stage-two peas? Aren't those for babies?" questions. Here he could be himself, and no one would judge his uniqueness. And even though she had not met our son, the teacher seemed to already care for him. That made me happy. I could not wait to see him blossom in his new surroundings. And blossom he did.

In that first year at his new school, he accomplished more than I ever imagined or had been told he would. Within just a few months, he was what we called daytime potty-trained. No longer did he need to wear pull-ups to school or during his days at the house. He had mastered going to pee, and he was proud of himself. We still (and continue to) had problems with bowel movements and overnight accidents, but I have no doubt that one day that will also be a thing of the past. Before he started kindergarten, he was a boy of few words. So when his teacher said to me, "We are going to start sending sight words / beginner words home with him. I believe he is ready to start reading," I was shocked.

My response was, "Are you sure? He can't even hold a pencil."

His teacher politely laughed and said, "He does not need to know how to write for him to read." I had to think about that for a minute. When I was younger, we had to learn to write first. Then we moved onto learning to read. I just assumed that was how things were still done. I am thankful times have changed. I am grateful for the teachers who now work with the child's abilities versus following some "this is how it must be done" format. We had focused so much of our time on the basics like holding a pencil or crayon and worried because he could not; the thought of him reading seemed impossible. I felt like I had failed him. Much to our delight and amazement, he did start to read a few months after the words started coming home. And by midyear, he was trying, somewhat successfully, to hold a pencil and could write his name and most of the alphabet. This school changed him in a positive way. The shy little boy who had started out that year was no more. He was confident in his newfound abilities. I know his preschool teachers loved him, but they did not have the resources available for what he needed. They did the best they could with what they had to work with. They gave him the foundation and the confidence to become the success he is today. I still send them updates when he does something new and exciting. And even though they miss seeing him in the halls of the school, they all know that the move was the best thing for him. God placed us where we needed to be in order to give JR a chance to succeed. He is not the same child who moved here. I have new hope for his future. I love seeing him prove the doctors and others wrong every time he does something they thought he would never do.

When Elissa came to us, she was sixteen months old. Her connection with her birth mom was little to none. So it was no surprise that when she came into our care, she wanted nothing to do with me. Without a mother figure in her life, she did not connect with me as well as the other children who had been in and out of our home had. I longed for a more personal relationship with her, but no matter how hard I tried, she never wanted that mommy/daughter scenario with me. She was going to be a daddy's girl, and I was fine with that. My top priority was to make sure she felt loved and safe in our home.

Around the age of four, her withdrawal from others became more noticeable and her behavior became worse. She started acting out more at the house and at her preschool. At home, if she was not getting her way, she would pee her pants or hit her head against the floor or wall. At night, she would walk the hall or talk to herself. Many nights, I went in her room to tell her to go to sleep, only to find out she was indeed asleep, just talking to herself. We joked that she had too much to say in the day that she had to finish her thoughts in her sleep. We assumed things would get better, but things only got worse. By the time she made it to kindergarten, she was not following the class rules and was talking back to the teacher, cutting her hair and face with scissors in art class, writing on desks, and taking things that did not belong to her. I talked to a few people, close friends and family, about her behavior, and I got the "Well, she has been through a lot in her short little life. I'm sure she will outgrow it" speech in some form. No one wanted to think something was wrong with her. I know I didn't want to think so. But I knew her behavior was not typical, no matter what her background. I didn't know who to call or who to talk to, so I called the one person I trusted to give me a straight answer. I made an appointment with her pediatrician.

Her pediatrician was more like family than a doctor to us. Her children and my older children were the same age. We had become friends over our twenty-plus years of doctor visits. She had been there through it all. She had seen us through Sierra's hip issues when she was born, Devin's surgeries stemming from Hirschberg's disease, his broken wrist, their countless ear infections, numerous strep throat trips, and routine well-child visits. So, when we became foster parents, she was more than willing to see our new children. I voiced my concerns about Elissa's behavior to her, and she agreed that given her background and her increased behaviors, she could benefit from seeing a therapist. The referral was made, and within a few weeks, on Monday morning I found myself in a small room discussing my daughter's peculiar behavior with a gentleman I had just met. She sat on the floor, all smiles, while I answered questions about her life at home and her past. She was in her own little world. She started kicking at the couch and yelling it was time to go home. I told her to stop, but she did not listen. When the therapist told her we were still talking, she became angry. Really angry. Dare I say it, but I was glad she acted that way. She was good at "acting golden" in front of other people; it's no wonder most people did not believe us when we told them what was going on at home. At five, she was a master manipulator. So, I found her outburst refreshing in an odd way. What I didn't expect was her treatment. I don't know what I expected exactly, but I was not impressed. Over the next few weeks, we were asked to work on things like sharing and learning to tell the difference between a truth and a lie. While we did as the new therapist asked, I knew we were way past the sharing is caring aspect of her treatment. She needed help.

My husband moved to Tennessee for his job early in her therapy sessions. Her behavior only escalated after he relocated. I felt all alone with a child who disliked me at best most days. Plus, I still had all our other children to care for. What had I gotten myself into? What had I gotten our family into? Her adoption was final, so there was no turning back. She was ours, we loved her, and we had to figure this out together. We had to work through the problems to find a solution. I thought I was prepared to handle anything. I had, after all, already raised two well-adjusted children. But it turns out one can't be prepared for everything, and I quickly learned they did not cover everything in those early foster care classes. She may be my child now, but she reminded me daily I was not her "real mom."

We continued therapy, but by this time, I had people telling me her behavior was surely the result of her dad taking the new job and being away so much. That might have been partly true, but she was acting out long before he had left. I could not do much of anything with her. She would scream daily as I brushed her hair and make up lies about our other children. She was caught by her teacher eating pencil erasers, and when asked why she was doing so, she said she had to because we didn't feed her. She started biting herself and blaming her younger siblings. If she was caught doing something she was not supposed to be doing, she would throw her head against the wall. I was grateful that Devin was there to help out on the really hard days. I was thankful when we finally moved. At least I would have her dad to help when we went into these self-destructive fits. Maybe a change in her surroundings was just what she needed.

After the move, Elissa settled into her new school and her new classroom, but it was not easy for her. The new teacher quickly picked up on her behaviors. Within the first few weeks, she had walked out of class, cut her hair … again, written her name on the carpet, and refused to follow any of the class rules. The other students distanced themselves from her and labeled her a "bad kid" and a "bully." Our daughter, the smallest in the class and barely forty pounds, had become the new bully in the class. Not exactly the way we wanted to start off at the new school. She was lost, and we had nowhere to turn. Our nights were exhausting and heartbreaking. It was as if she knew what she was doing but had no control over her actions. At home, she had created a fairy-tale world with her and her "real mom." She told me stories of how the two of them loved going to the movies and eating popcorn. She even talked about going trick-or-treating with her and how they loved staying up late watching TV, none of which ever happened. Everything she talked about doing with her real mom she had done with me, but it was clear she did not see me as her mom. We were referred to a therapist, and I prayed he or she would listen. And she did.

From the moment we walked in, the new therapist listened to my concerns and to what Elissa had to say. She used toys to get through to Elissa and talked on a level she was able to understand. I was pleased. As the visits went on, the therapist conducted some tests to see what was going on. It was later determined that our daughter suffered from FASD (fetal alcohol spectrum disorder) / RAD (reactive attachment disorder) / ADD and ADHD. I was relieved we finally had a diagnosis but scared at what the diagnosis was. With the way she took everything out on me and not my husband, the way she refused to listen to anyone in authority, and the disconnect from those who loved her, the RAD made sense. As for the FASD diagnosis, she had some of the characteristics. They were mild but still there. We knew of the drug use while her mother was pregnant, so it was possible she used alcohol as well.

I was met with the concerns from family about starting her on medicine. I did not personally want to start her on medicine either, but we had to do something. The lies, stealing, and her behavior were getting to be more than we could handle, and it was disrupting our home and our lives. It was hard for those who did not live day to day with her to see the problems. But at home, the problems continued to grow. Thankfully, we found help. Over time, we found the right combination of medicines, and her behavior, although not perfect, did gradually improve. We still deal with more difficult days than most people, but we are managing much better now. And while she still fantasizes about her birth mom from time to time, our bond has become stronger. She knows how much I love her, and from time to time, she lets me know she loves me also. And though they are few and far between, we have even enjoyed a few mommy and daughter moments.

Now back to our story. Before we knew it, summer was over, and time had come to tell Sierra goodbye. She packed up her Jeep and headed back to college. We were now six hours away from her, so her coming home on the weekends was not going to happen as much as it did before. She would start her senior year at Davis and Elkins college that fall, and she would quickly become busy with senior projects, debates, and her final thesis. I know we would not see much of her, which only made goodbye that much harder.

For the first time since we became a forever family to our five little loves, Todd and I were completely on our own with them. No longer would we have Sierra or Devin watch the kids while we ran to the store or if we wanted a date night. Our little ones went with us or we didn't go. The kids missed going to their grandparents' to visit on the weekends, and I missed my afternoon movies and coffee with my friends. On more than one occasion, I found myself wanting to pack everything and everyone back up and move back to the only place I had ever called home. The first few months left me to wonder if we had really made the right call. I felt so alone, even with all my children and husband around me.

But life moved on. We became friends with a few couples from church and with Todd's boss's family, and things started to feel more like home. We were now going to church on Sunday mornings and to small group on Wednesdays nights. Small group quickly became one of my favorite parts of the week. The adults had Bible study while the kids enjoyed music and movies. It was refreshing to be able to go somewhere we all enjoyed. We slowly started making Tennessee our home. All the worries about the move slowly faded away.

One afternoon, Elissa and I sat at the dining room table while she ate her after-school snack. The boys and Sadie were in the living room playing with cars. As she chewed her peanut butter sandwich and drank her milk, she talked about what she had done at school and about her upcoming dance practice. Out of nowhere, she looked up at me and said, "Hey, Mom, I talked to God last night."

"You did, did you?" I chuckled. "I'm guessing you said some extra prayers with Daddy last night?"

"Yes, but that's not what I mean. I mean I really talked to God last night. He told me all about my new sister, Eden Grace." You could have heard a pin drop. For once in my life, I was speechless, so I let her talk. "Yeah, He says she is going to be my new sister. But don't worry, Momma. We have time to get things in order. He says she won't get here for a few more years. Oh, Mommy, she is so pretty. We are going to be the best of friends."

She then took another bite of her sandwich, and I managed to take a drink of my water. "Sweetie, Daddy and Mommy aren't expecting any more babies or kids. Are you sure that's what you heard?" I was still in disbelief that this was the conversation we were having over chips and peanut butter sandwiches.

"I'm sure, Momma. He said not to worry. He had it all worked out." She finished up her milk and asked to be excused. I sat there for several minutes trying to process what had just taken place.

I could have dismissed the whole conversation as a little girl's wild imagination, and with her gift of telling stories, it would have been easy to do. However, something about the way she said it made me wonder. I have had talks with God about many things, including our son Alex, so why would Elissa's conversation with God be any different? After my husband came home and he had finished dinner, I told him about my afternoon chat with our daughter. I figured he would shake his head no and say something along the lines, "Are you completely out of your mind?" seeing that we were now down here without any help from our family. But he didn't. He did sit quietly for a few minutes and then looked over at me. "So, we have a few years, do we? If it's something you want to consider, then I guess we better. I'm okay with helping out a few more." How did I get blessed with such a big-hearted man?

The next morning, I found myself researching the ins and outs of foster care in the state of Tennessee. The new journey, however, was short-lived. In order to become foster parents, you had to be a resident of the state for more than six months. While Todd had been here long enough, the kids and I had not. I took it as a sign that it was not meant to be and put the idea of becoming a foster parent out of my mind.

We celebrated our first holiday season complete with Halloween costumes and candy, a family Thanksgiving dinner, and Christmas. The kids were more than excited at Christmas. Both my parents and my in-laws traveled down Christmas Day to see us and make our first Tennessee Christmas a success. The kids spent most of the morning opening presents and eating Christmas cookies. We had a traditional Christmas dinner complete with turkey, ham, mashed potatoes, and of course mac-n-cheese for the kids. Both grandmothers enjoyed the handmade ornaments the kids had made them.

For my dad, I finished a quilt. In the move, I had discovered a quilt top my dad's mom had completed before she passed away in August 1990. It had been stored away for years and nearly forgotten. When I unpacked it, I knew I had to finish it. It was the perfect gift to give him now that we had moved. Seeing that our newest daughter was named after her, I knew my grandma would appreciate me finishing it. I am sure she was smiling down on me as I worked on it. A few of the blocks had to be replaced, but in the end, the quilt had turned out better than I expected. The smile on my parents' face said it all.

The holidays passed, and we moved into winter. One January morning while Elissa was rushing around to get dressed for school, she brought up Eden Grace. "Mom, will Eden share a room with me or will she share a room with Sadie? Or will Sadie and I share a room and Eden get one to herself?"

I was stopped in my tracks. I thought we had moved past her longing for a new sister. I should have answered differently, but I said something like, "Sweetie, I don't think we need to worry about that. There are no new kids coming to stay with us." As I said those words, however, my mind was figuring out who would go in what bedroom and who I thought would work better as roommates.

The truth is I missed foster care. I missed helping children. I missed the people. I missed making a difference. I had considered becoming a CASA (court appointed special advocate) worker, but that's not where my heart lied. I still felt we were needed on the front lines as the children came in to care. After a few days of pondering the idea, I went back to the computer and located two different foster care agencies. I called and left messages at both places for someone to call me back. The next day, a worker from the specialized foster care agency called me back. As I talked with her, she told me they work solely with children who have major medical needs. With this agency, our training from West Virginia would not be transferable. We would have to take a thirty-hour training class along with classes that specialized in the medical needs of severely disabled children. As badly as I wanted to help out, I knew that was not something we were capable of doing at that time. She thanked me for calling and said that if we changed our minds to give her a call back.

A few days later, the phone rang, and it was a worker from the DCS office. We made small talk, and she asked me how we came to the decision of wanting to be foster parents. So, I gave her a brief rundown of our history as foster parents back in West Virginia and told her that we still felt we were meant to help in some way. She asked about our training, and I provided her with all the information she needed. We went over the numbers and seeing that we already have five children in our home, we would only be able to foster one child at a time, given the state's six children max rule. She was excited and seemed to think we could still be valuable to the agency. She did, however, warn me that she was not sure if our training would carry over. She would need to check with her supervisor and let us know.

I checked back with her a few times after that, only to find out that she had not heard back from anyone. I did not want to become a bother, and by this point, I knew it was completely out of my hands. If it was meant to be, God would make a way. Todd and I discussed things, and if we were required to retake the thirty-hour training, we would not be able to become foster parents here, not now anyway. Maybe when the kids were older. Although we had made a few new friends, I still didn't feel comfortable having anyone watch the kids while we spent time at training. And having our parents or older children come down that much to watch them was not an option.

But when God has a plan, He makes a way. We were already in March before the email came in. "Hey, I finally heard back from the supervisors. I have great news. We can use your training classes for West Virginia. All we need to do is a home study and a refresher CPR class. Call me and we will set one up."

I could not believe it. I thought our journey as foster parents had ended with our move. Once again, God had taken the impossible and made it possible. As I marked the calendar with the upcoming date for the CPR class, I could feel a smile come across my face. God still wanted to use us. I could not help but think back to the conversation Elissa and I had about Eden Grace. I was not sure if she was part of God's plan for us, but at least I knew we were going to be given to the chance to help another child. At that moment, I stopped and prayed. Tears ran down my face. *We will follow You, oh Lord, wherever You lead us. Thy will be done in our lives.* I stood there in my kitchen for the next twenty to thirty minutes and just gave Him praise. God had been so good to us along this journey, and it was by His grace we were not finished.

March was a busy month at our home. After countless meetings, lost school files, retesting and months of waiting, Alex and Eli were finally cleared to go to preschool. They had missed a great deal of the year, so the teacher and I agreed they would attend five days a week from 8:00 to 1:30. During the testing, a concern arose with Alex. We knew he was not talking as much as the typical three-and-a-half-year-old should, but when we saw his scores, we knew it was worse than we thought. After yet another meeting, it was suggested we test him to see if he also had autism. Although getting him into preschool took months, scheduling the autism test happened in less than a week. We found ourselves at the psychologist's office on Thursday morning. I was afraid Alex would be too shy to participate in the testing, but the therapist made him feel comfortable, and he did as well as any three-and-a-half-year-old would do. She asked me questions, and I gave her the answers. All in all, the visit went well. All we had to do was wait for the results. If he was autistic, he would receive more services at school. If it came back he was not on the autism spectrum and that it was classified as a learning delay, that also would be addressed in school. Either way, he would still be my beautiful, dark-haired, brown-eyed boy.

As we waited for Alex's results, we managed to attend our refresher CPR class and a class on how to give medication. Our home study was completed, and our children were interviewed. Questionnaires were sent out to our references, fingerprints were done, and all the necessary paperwork was filled out. All we had to do now was wait and see if we were needed in Tennessee. Waiting. The all-familiar part of foster care.

Being a Voice for Foster Care

As foster parents, we are asked to not only care for the basic needs of a child, but also to sit alongside them as they digest the hurt and damage they have undeservingly experienced.
—Carrie Dahlin

Being a voice for those that have none. That's part of being a foster parent. Early on in our foster care journey when someone would ask, "Are they twins?" or "Are they all yours?" or even when people just looked at our beautiful chaos while we were at the store, it was an opportunity to tell them about foster care. I used every opportunity I ran across to promote being a foster parent. The children needed a voice. The world of foster care is often overlooked and almost always misunderstood. One of my favorite things was taking a part on the panel at new foster parent trainings. The panel normally consisted of a few seasoned foster parents, a caseworker, an adoption worker, and a supervisor from the department. I remember the first panel we were asked to speak at. I was a nervous wreck. What would I say? Would they even ask us anything? What if I didn't have the answer they were looking for? What if our story changed their minds about being foster parents? My husband was his usual calm self. We arrived at the college, the same college where we had taken our training classes and went up to the training hall. There we were greeted by our former trainer with a warm smile and a welcome hug. I looked out at the class and remembered what I felt like when I was in their shoes. We made small talk with the trainer and with the other panelists and then took our seats in the front of the class. The trainer had us introduce ourselves and then asked us to give a little background about why we decided to become foster or foster-to-adopt parents.

One by one, we went down the line of panelists. The caseworker talked about why she had decided to become a social worker, the adoption worker talked about the joys of making forever families for kids who needed a home, and our trainer talked about the strength and devotion it took to care for the children in foster care. Then came our turn. My husband looked at me and said, "Go ahead. You tell it better." So, I started by introducing us and gave a little background on our forever family while my husband sat and nodded along. After introductions, the class was allowed to ask us questions. A few who wanted to adopt worried about becoming too attached to a child that they might have to give back. Others asked questions about how long the process took from start to finish. Some asked about the money. As we sat there listening to the questions and even getting to answer a few, I caught myself scanning the group as I imagine the panel from our training class did. I wondered which ones would go on and be wonderful foster parents. I wondered which ones would start, only to become overwhelmed and quit. I wondered with this group how many children would find their forever homes.

We asked for final questions, and with that, our first panel session was complete. The trainer hugged us and thanked us for coming. I told her if she ever needed us again to just call. And she smiled. "I'll be in contact with you from time to time I'm sure. Excellent job. Thanks for coming out." I have lost track of how many panels we took part in over the years.

Our local foster/ foster-to-adopt support group was also a huge part of our lives. This was (still is) a group of foster parents that met once a month for training, fellowship, and to support each other. It was an effortless way to keep up with the required training hours as well as being a wonderful place to vent, ask questions, and be surrounded by other people who understood all the ups and downs that come with foster care. Our group consisted of about thirty adults and their children. Training covered anything from how to maintain healthy hygiene to how to help a child cope while their parents are in jail. The group not only provided the necessary training we needed, but it was also a place where we could plan different activities for the kids in foster care. Throughout the years, the group hosted pool parties, cookouts, Halloween parties, and everyone's favorite, the annual Christmas party. It was a safe place for the kids to enjoy being kids. The activities were used to get to know each other better and to allow us to fellowship outside of the trainings. I served as the treasurer for a little over a year and then was elected president of the group for a term. I would have loved to have kept going but resigned when elections rolled around because I knew I would not be around the following year because of our move to Tennessee. The group quickly became a second family. Many of the parents there had both biological children and foster children just like us. Some had adopted out of foster care, while others were strictly foster parents. Some had only one child, while others had eight. We were all different yet all the same. Our desire to help the children in need made us family. We understood what a call at 2:00 a.m. was like. We understood what it felt like to have a child reunified after they had been part of the family for close to two years. We laughed together and cried together, and some of us even prayed together. Some of my closest friends come from this group.

One of my passions is helping others become foster parents. I love helping someone thinking about foster care work through the process to become a foster parent. I love answering questions and showing potentially new foster parents how to sign up and how to get started. When we started, we had no one pointing us in the right direction. We just went with it and hoped for the best. I would have loved if someone had told us what we could expect and to have shown us the ropes. So, when people call me, text me, or message me, I try my best to help them out. Many people that have asked have gone on to become foster parents, and some have gone on to be adoptive parents, and that makes me happy. On my mom's side of the family, we have added sixteen new additions to our family through foster care adoptions. God has blessed our family and our extended family time after time with the joy of adoption. I also have several close friends who have been blessed with new additions to their families through foster care. So yes, I have a lot to be thankful for, and I tell as many as I can about our journey, hoping they might feel the need to help as well. I have written letters to try to make changes in our laws, and I have taken part in walks to raise awareness. And yet there is still more to do to raise foster care awareness. That's where the idea for this book came from. Over the last few years, I have been asked to share our story by writing a book. The only problem is I am not a writer. But here we are. I started putting my thoughts together a little over a year ago and stopped because I just didn't feel I was qualified. It was just a childish dream, I thought to myself. Then a dear friend of mine reminded me of one of my favorite scriptures; God does not call the qualified; He qualifies the called. I'm so thankful for that friend and her encouraging words.

Where Are We Now?

Many things have changed since our first placement came through our door in November 2010. We are now a family of nine. We have fostered over twenty-five children and have adopted five. Our oldest daughter, Sierra, recently graduated from college, with double major in political science and English, and has taken a job close to Washington, DC. She loves working with the children God has placed in her path. I think she misses being around her siblings, and in some way, teaching reminds her of them. She continues to take her role as Big Sissy very seriously and calls to chat with the kids a few times a week. I can't wait to see what the future holds for her. Our son Devin attends college back in West Virginia and works full-time at a local fast-food restaurant. He is pursuing a teaching degree and hopes to become a high school history teacher. He still helps over at taekwondo teaching the next generation of gups (students) the way of the hand and foot. He and Sierra are the highest-ranking siblings at the school. He is a third-degree black belt, and she is a fourth-degree black belt. We are looking forward to watching him test for his fourth degree as soon as he is old enough. Not having them here in Tennessee is hard on me, but I am so proud of the young adults they have become. It's their time to shine, following their own dreams. I know they will be just fine. And they know if they need me, I am just a phone call away.

Elissa is now in second grade. We have seen some progress with her medicine, and dare I say, we are looking forward to a better year next year. She is such a bright child who loves to read and dance. She is eager to share her room with the next little girl God sends our way. We are working on our mother-daughter relationship, and we are doing better. We are taking it day by day. There is a twinkle in her eyes now that we have not seen before. I am hopeful that means better days are coming her way. She deserves the best out of life.

JR is now in first grade. He will be in between the autism classroom and a regular classroom with an aide this year. He has taken over our breakfast nook and calls it his office. It is filled with all his treasures. There are Legos, cars, construction paper, crayons, and empty pizza boxes. His "coworkers," as he calls them, are his Five Nights of Freddy's action figures. He can spend hours playing by himself in there. Keeping clothes on him is still a challenge, but we are working on it. His world is hard for people to understand; some have stopped interacting with us altogether because it's too difficult for them, and I get it. Its hard. But there is so much more to him than just his autism diagnosis. They can choose to not be in his bright, beautiful world, but there's no place I'd rather be. God made JR perfect in His image, and we are blessed to have him in our lives.

Alex was diagnosed with sensory processing disorder and will be seeing a geneticist in the near future. He has started saying a few words and continues to dazzle us with his electric personality. He is so full of life. He loves to play with his dinosaurs and loves to dress up like his favorite superheroes. He is also a huge helper in the kitchen. He is excited about preschool this year. He has grown into a fine little man. Eli is also in preschool. He loves to learn new things and enjoys coming home and telling us all about his day. His new favorite subject is sign language. He can sign the alphabet both forward and backwards. He is our class clown and makes us laugh every day. He lets everyone know he's momma's baby boy, a title he wears proudly. He can already write his name, and he knows all his colors and shapes. He is a little obsessed with the new movie *Disney*

Cars 3 right now. He can tell you all their names and sing all the songs. He is definitely growing into his own person.

As for Sadie, well she's two and is into everything. She is such a happy little girl. She loves to dance and play peek-a-boo. Thanks to her brothers, she is already counting and working on her alphabet. She greets each morning with her beautiful smile and fights sleep like a champ. I think she's afraid she will miss something if she goes to sleep. She is such a blessing to us.

Also, an update on a few of our previous foster kids. God had plans for them as well.

It took a few months, but the aunt to our first set of sisters and I became friends on a social media site. I think both families needed a little time to get use to God's permanent plan for the girls. The aunt (now their forever mom) and I talk often. Thanks to today's technology, I get to see those precious little girls grow up. Thank You, Jesus, for that. They are growing into fine, beautiful, and talented young ladies. They may never know how they touched our lives or how much to this day we love them, but they are forever in our hearts. And who knows—maybe one day when they are old enough to understand what happened, we will get to see them face-to-face again. I pray that prayer daily. Until then, I wish them happiness and love. I am so thankful we had them for the time God intended. We do not always understand the storm we face in life or understand why things happen the way they do, but God knows. And as long as He is in control, things will work out. We just have to have faith.

The brothers we had were adopted by the family they went to live with after leaving our house. The family was also able to later adopt the boys' sister, who was born after they moved into their home. Their forever mom and I are still good friends and talk often. In fact, my parents played Santa and Mrs. Claus for their family's Christmas party last year. My parents loved seeing the boys again, even if the boys had no clue who they were. They are doing amazing in their new life and are very active in sports and other activities. I love seeing updates on them. I can't believe how much they have changed. They are so happy and right where God intended them to be.

The girls stayed with Jon and Nadine for about seven months before they were reunified with their biological father and stepmom. The stepmom sends updates to Nadine, so I still get to see and hear what's happening with them. They are both doing well in school and are enjoying being big sisters to their new baby brother. As for Jon and Nadine, after the girls were reunified, they received a call for a Safe Haven baby that is now their beautiful daughter. Her adoption was final a little over a year ago. I got to help pick out her middle name. She is so precious. Nadine has become one of my dearest friends. We both have moved out of West Virginia but continue to talk regularly and cheer on our Green Bay Packers through text and Facebook posts. I am also happy to report that after trying to conceive a baby for fifteen years, Nadine and Jon welcomed a healthy, beautiful baby girl this past November, making them a very blessed family of four. God is so good to those who are patient and faithful.

We will all be forever connected. These children, their parents, all our foster children we had the privilege to foster, and their parents will always be in our hearts. They are part of our extended family. It may not have been God's plan for the children to stay with us, but it was His plan for our families to cross paths. I am so honored to be part of this beautiful masterpiece He has created.

As for me, I have grown as a person. I forgave the truck driver that changed the direction of my life. In an odd way, he made this life possible for me to have. It's funny how things work out. Living a life so full of hate and anger about something I had no control over did not suit me well. I have also forgiven those from my past that hurt me; not for their benefit but for mine. I needed closure in order to be happy and move forward with my life. God gave me such peace after I decided to forgive and move forward. I am also currently waiting to have another surgery on my back. My SCS batteries did not last the six years as the doctor had hoped. It's a never-ending process. My injuries keep me grounded in my faith and remind me I need God to make it through each and every day. I continue to look forward to a day when surgery is no longer needed. After all, I still believe in miracles. Until then, I have seven reasons to keep moving forward, and I will do whatever necessary to stay as healthy as possible for them. My back will heal, and the scars will fade. I am blessed to be married to my best friend, my wonderful husband Todd. He has been by my side throughout this whole journey. He never questioned our roles in God's plan for us. I know that if a call comes in he will say *Yes, What's one more?* To have a man with such a companionate heart is truly a blessing. Thank you, Jesus, for a second chance at happiness.

As for our family, we have adjusted to life in Tennessee. We are making the most out of the blessings God has given us. Todd now holds a new inside sales position at his company. He still drives a truck from time to time when they need him, but he is settling into his new position, and we love having him home more. Some of our days are great, while others are filled with meltdowns. With five children under the age of seven, you can always expect something to be going on. But we would not trade our life for anything. God did not promise every day would be sunshine and rainbows, but He did promise to walk with us and guide us every step of the way. I am thankful for that promise. He has been with us each day, and for that I am truly grateful.

As for our Tennessee foster care journey, we have taken a few calls. We have learned what we can handle and what we cannot. We still have the extra bedroom fixed up in neutral colors. There is a toy box full of cars, dolls, and puzzles just in case they are needed. We have totes full of clothing ranging from newborn to preteen in both boys and girls. We have extra blankets and pillows ready to use for those middle-of-the-night calls. We are ready if God decides He needs us again. Many judge us for taking in more children, and my reply to them is this. Knowing what we know now, seeing what we see on the news and hear about on social media, how can they expect us *not* to help? The need is real. The need is growing. We know the price we will pay, but we fear the price the children will pay if someone does not step up to help them when their world is crumbling around them. We will be here if God sees fit to use us for the next child who is hurting, the next child who needs a place to sleep, and the next child who needs to eat. We will comfort them, love them, protect them, help them, and hold them. This is our beautiful chaos. This is our life.

Foster Agencies in West Virginia

Necco
www.necco.org
Huntington office 304-733-0036
Cross Lanes office 304-759-9835
Logan office 304-752-7830
Children's Home Society West Virginia
www.childhswv.org
Princeton office 304-431-2424
Charleston office 304-345-3894
Huntington office 304-743-2345
Mission West Virginia
www.missionwv.org
1-866-CALL-MWV
Hurricane office 304-562-0723
Frameworks through Mission West Virginia
KVC of West Virginia
www.westvirginiakvc.org
Charleston office 304-347-9818
Jackson County office 304-373-1108
Raleigh County office 304-929-4130
You can also contact your local Department of Health and Human Resource (DHHR) office and ask about upcoming Pride Training classes in your area.

Foster Agencies in Tennessee

The Omni Family
www.omnifosteradoption.theomnifamily.com
NE Tennessee Regional office 423-913-2569
Middle Tennessee Regional office 615-834-1885 or 888-742-3905
New Beginnings
www.newbeginningsadoptions.org
Tennessee office 1-615-378-7099
Camelot
www.thecamelotdifference.com
Nashville, Tennessee 615-678-6283
Kingsport, Tennessee 423-392-2975
Clarksville, Tennessee 931-304-2555
You can also contact your local Department of Children Services (DCS) and ask about upcoming Path Training classes.
National site
Dave Thomas Foundation
www.davethomasfoundation.org   or   call   1-800-ASK-DTFA (1-800-275-3832)

Our three plus one became a family. Our wedding day.

Elissa and JR's adoption day September 2013

Little Miss meeting Wild Man for the first time

Celebrating the news of their upcoming adoption
at Disney World with Mamaw Deb

The kids on our first vacation as a family of six

Adoption announcement photo for Alex and Eli June 2015. Photo credit Cierra Spaulding Photography

First beach trip for Big Al and Elmo June 2014

My Green Bay Packer twins ready to watch the game

My parents, Papaw Rick and Mamaw Deb, with Alex and Eli on their adoption day June 2015

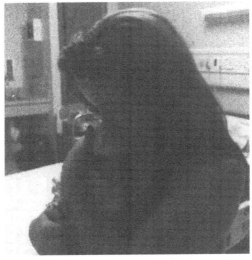

Big Sissy meeting baby Peanut aka baby Sadie for the first time

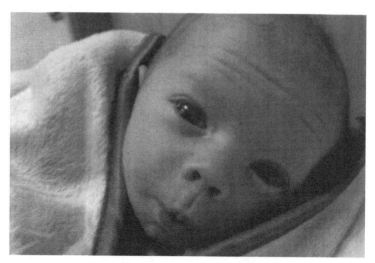

Peanut the day she came home

Sadie's first birthday photos. She is wearing her Great-Grandmother Sadie's apron and pearls.

Our little loves first Christmas in Tennessee

Sadie surrounded by love from her grandparents on her adoption day

Our beautiful chaos. All nine of us on Sadie's adoption day June 2016

JR by the tree our first Christmas in Tennessee

Sierra and Devin. They are the highest-ranking siblings at their dojang. She is a fourth-degree black belt. He is a third-degree black belt.

Big Bubby aka Devin enjoying some beach time with his little siblings

My in-laws, Papaw Jim and Mamaw Sue enjoying a day at the beach with the kids

Big Sissy aka Sierra posing for a photo with her younger siblings at the zoo

Our Super Heroes

Our Beautiful Chaos. Photo credit Cierra Spaulding Photography

My world. My life. My family. Photo credit Cierra Spaulding Photography

Photo credit JR Smith